GRIMM TALES

adapted from the Brothers Grimm
by Carol Ann Duffy

dramatized by Tim Supple

faber and faber

LONDON · BOSTON

First published in 1996
by Faber and Faber Limited
3 Queen Square London WC1N 3AU

Photoset by Wilmaset Ltd, Birkenhead, Wirral
Printed in England by
Mackays of Chatham PLC, Chatham, Kent

Dramatization and Notes © Tim Supple, 1996
Adaptation © Carol Ann Duffy, 1996
Illustrations © Melany Still, 1996

A CIP record for this book
is available from the British Library

ISBN 0-571-17677-1

4 6 8 10 9 7 5

Grimm Tales

Carol Ann Duffy was born in Glasgow in 1955. After reading Philosophy at Liverpool University she moved to London, where she now lives. Her *Selected Poems* are published by Penguin and her poetry has received several awards in Britain and America, including the Whitbread and Foward prizes in 1993 and the Lannan Literary Award in 1995. She has one small daughter.

Tim Supple is Artistic Director of the Young Vic. His work for the company includes *Omma, The Slab Boys Trilogy* and *Grimm Tales*. He has also directed at York Theatre Royal, Leicester Haymarket, Sheffield Crucible, the Royal National Theatre and most recently for the Royal Shakespeare Company.

Contents

Grimm Tales was first produced at the Young Vic
Theatre, London, on 23 November 1994. The company
were:

Alan Perrin, Dan Milne, Paul M. Meston, Rory Murrary,
Linda Kerr Scott, Sarah C. Cameron, Natasha Pope

Musicians Adrian Lee, Sylvia Hallet, Dawson Ben
Hassine-Miller

Directed by Tim Supple
Designed by Melany Still
Music by Adrian Lee
Lighting by Chris Davey
Puppets by Miles and Jak
Movement Direction by Melany Still
Research by Sue Emmas
Associate Designer Mike Bailey

Notes

Grimm Tales has two scripts: the uncut versions of the stories Carol Ann Duffy wrote for us, which provided the text for rehearsals, and the text we created through rehearsal and performance. Our aim was to find the most direct theatrical adaptation we could for each story. We therefore asked Carol Ann, a poet, not to make any theatrical adaptations. Her work was to draw from each story its particular linguistic qualities and to give the language the simple rhythms of speech. Our task was then to give each story its particular theatrical shape. Decisions on who would speak and who would do what were based partly on our perceptions of the style or form demanded by each story and partly on the particular talents of the performers in our company. We found we did not need any formal means of tying the stories together, no frame or thread or justification was necessary: the collection itself, the event of one group telling all the stories, was enough. The stage is the setting, the atmosphere of the stories is the cement, and the audience's imagination provides the rest.

TEXT

We have tried to lay out the performance script to give a suggestion of rhythm and episode. Similarly, we have used punctuation differently in different stories to suggest the varying patterns of speech. It should be clear that narration works unselfconsciously as a part of dialogue. Sometimes a narrator stands back from the action (as in *The Golden Goose*); sometimes narration functions entirely as dialogue (as in *Hansel and Gretel*); and sometimes both approaches are combined (as in *Ashputtel*). The aim is always that the audience should notice nothing but the story. If narration feels like dialogue and dialogue like narration, the script will live.

There are many inconsistencies between the original stories and the theatre text. The originals are verbatim from Grimm; the theatre texts represent either a response to the rhythms of performance (for example, the lessening or editing of repetitions), or our own instincts on particular matters (for example, the stepmother in the Grimms' *Hansel and Gretel* becomes the mother in ours – the brothers heard the story as the mother and themselves invented the step . . .).

We have inserted stage directions only where strictly necessary. Most of the time the narrative itself provides a full guide to entrances, exits, places and objects. The solutions to the physical demands of the stories must be particular to each group that chooses to tell them.

DESIGN

The original production was played in the round with no setting and very few props. The stage floor provided the background – thick planks with the bark of the tree and the grain clearly visible. Two traps in the floor were used sparingly: as the shed and oven in *Hansel and Gretel* and the pool in *Iron Hans*. The design created a distinct world of costume and colour in each story; the clothes were always simple in line and pattern. In the Grimms' tales the supernatural and the fantastic are always found in the real and ordinary made extreme, and the design reflected this. Sources were wide-ranging but always European and rich in refined reality. The simplicity and clarity of wood engravings were generally influential: the haunting pictures of Käthe Kollwitz provided inspiration for *Hansel and Gretel*; the paintings of Brueghel for *The Golden Goose* and *The Magic Table, The Gold-Donkey*

and The Cudgel in the Sack; the strange meeting-points
of Asiatic Europe for *Ashputtel*. We steered a path well
clear of the vision of fairly tales found in pantomime and
Disney films: the Grimms' are as much folk as fairy
stories. Props and clothes reappeared when necessary,
and so the design provided an important homogeneity as
well as a narrative clarity in each story. Lighting was also
distinct – striking though unfussy. Whatever the
circumstances of the productions, whatever the physical
staging, the most important relationship is between the
stories and the audience. Everything else – actors, design,
music, staging – is simply a means to communicate these
serious, ancient and remarkable narratives.

MUSIC

Our company included three musicians, present
throughout rehearsals and playing live. The musical
accompaniment was continuous. They played:

Player 1 'ud, mandola, sitar, tam-tam, crotales, bell tree,
Chinese cymbal, kendhang liblon, kendhang
ageng, kendhang gender.

Player 2 Vocals, violin, hurdy-gurdy, kemanche,
trombone, khene, Jew's harp, anklung, dai.

Player 3 Percussion: darbouka, bendir, bass drum
(Rajasthan), log drums, Tibetan singing bowl,
Ghanaian cowbell, Brazilian double bells, two
Thai gongs, African basket shaker, Brazilian metal
maracas, Nubian *tar* framed drums, Egyptian
mazhai frame drum, three Moroccan *tarija*,
assorted bird whistles, Bulgarian goat-bell, egg
shaker, American flat set of tom-toms, ship bells.

A full score of the music is available, based on the
original production but arranged for conventional
Western instruments; a reduced score is also available for
companies with limited means (see page iv).

We performed with short breaks between the stories during which music was played – the music bridged the stories, but each one began with a fresh start. Each story wipes the slate clean of the last.

The stories were performed by seven actors – four men and three women. Their main roles in each story were:

Actor 1	*Hansel and Gretel*	Father
	The Golden Goose	Narrator
	Ashputtel	Stepmother
	Iron Hans	Hunter, Second King
	The Lady and the Lion	Father
	The Magic Table . . .	First Son
Actor 2	*Hansel and Gretel*	Hansel
	The Golden Goose	First Son, Second Daughter

Grimm Tales

dramatized by Tim Supple
drawings by Melany Still

HANSEL AND GRETEL

Hansel and Gretel has the structure of a nightmare. A few domestic objects – buckets, a knife, a blanket, a plate, a jug, an axe – create both the house and the forest and appear in the Witch's house. The Mother also reappears, grotesque, as the Witch. A chorus of three is always present, and active. The narration rebounds between the characters and is always an aspect of character; the characters narrate their own actions and so we can see their inner life. The story is one of starvation, terror and catharsis. The rhythms of speech are taut and violent, containing the fearful tensions and, finally, joyous release of the drama.

Father It was no more than once upon a time when a poor woodcutter lived in a small house at the edge of a huge, dark forest. Now, the woodcutter lived with his wife and his two young children – a boy called Hansel and a little girl called Gretel. It was hard enough for him to feed them all at the best of times – but these were the worst of times; times of famine and hunger and starvation; and the woodcutter was lucky if he could get his hands on even a simple loaf of bread. Night after hungry night, he lay in his bed next to his thin wife, and he worried so much that he tossed and he turned and he sighed and he mumbled and moaned and he just couldn't sleep at all.

'Wife, wife, wife. What are we going to do? How can we feed our two poor children when we've hardly enough for ourselves? Wife, wife, what can be done?'

And as he fretted and sweated in the darkness, back came the bony voice of his wife; a voice as fierce as famine.

Mother 'Listen to me, husband. Tomorrow at first light we'll take the children into the forest, right into the cold, black heart of it. We'll make a fire for them there and give them each one last morsel of bread. Then we'll pretend to go off to our work and we'll leave them there all by themselves. They'll never be able to find their way back home on their own. We'll be rid of them for good and only have to worry about feeding ourselves.'

Father 'No, no, wife, I can't do that. How could I have the heart to leave young Hansel and Gretel in the forest?

The wild beasts would soon sniff them out and eat them alive.'

Mother 'You fool, do you want all four of us to starve to death? You might as well start smoothing the wood for our coffins.'

Father And she gave the poor, heartsore woodcutter no peace until he agreed to do as she said.

Hansel Now, Hansel and Gretel had been so hungry that night that they hadn't been able to sleep either, and they'd heard every cruel word of their mother's terrible plan.

Gretel Gretel cried bitter, salt tears, and said to Hansel: 'Now we're finished.'

Hansel 'Don't cry, Gretel. Don't be sad. I'll think of a way to save us.'

And when their father and mother had finally gone to sleep, Hansel got up, put on his coat, opened the back door, and crept out into the midnight hour.

Outside. Bright light.

There was bright, sparkling moonlight outside and the white pebbles on the ground shone like silver coins and precious jewels. Hansel bent down and filled his empty pockets with as many pebbles as he could carry.

Inside.

'Don't worry, Gretel, you can go to sleep now. We'll be fine, I promise.' And he got back into bed.

Mother At dawn, before the sun had properly risen, their mother came and woke the two children.

'Get up, you lazy scraps, we're going into the forest to chop wood.'

Then she gave each of them a miserable mouthful of bread: 'There's your lunch; think yourselves lucky, and don't eat it all at once, because there's nothing else.'

Gretel Gretel put the bread in her apron pocket, because Hansel's pockets were crammed with pebbles.

Father Then the whole family set off along the path to the forest.

Along the path. Hansel keeps stopping and turning back. Finally:

'Hansel, what are you trailing behind for and looking at? Keep up with the rest of us.'

Hansel 'Sorry, father, I'm just looking back at my white kitten. It's sitting up there on our roof, saying goodbye.'

Mother 'You stupid boy, that's not your kitten. It's just the light of the morning sun glinting on the chimney. Now come on.'

Hansel But, of course, Hansel hadn't been looking at anything at all. He'd been throwing the white pebbles from his pocket on to the path.

The family go deeper into the dark heart of the forest.

Gretel The forest was immense and gloomy.

Father When they had reached the middle, the woodcutter said: 'Now Hansel, now Gretel, gather up some wood and I'll make a nice fire to keep you warm.'

Hansel Hansel and Gretel collected a big pile of firewood and when it was set alight and the flames were like burning tongues, their mother said:

Mother 'Now lie down by the fire and rest. We're going further into the forest to chop wood. When we're finished working, we'll come back and get you.'

Hansel The children sat by the fire, and when midday came, they chewed on their small portions of bread. They could hear the blows of a woodcutter's axe nearby and they thought that their father was close.

Mother But it wasn't an axe, it was just a branch that he had tied to an old, withered tree and the wind was blowing it to and fro, to and fro.

Hansel After they had waited and waited and waited, the children's eyes grew as heavy as worry and they fell fast asleep.

When at last they woke up, it was already pitch dark, darker than a nightmare.

Gretel 'How are we going to find our way out of this enormous forest?'

Hansel 'Just wait a bit till the moon rises, Gretel, then we'll find our way home all right.'

And when the moon had risen, casting its brilliant, magical light, Hansel took his little sister by the hand and followed the pebbles.

They shone like newly minted coins . . .

Gretel Like cats' eyes . . .

Hansel Like diamonds, and showed them the way. They walked all through the night, and at daybreak they knocked on the door of their father's house.

They knock at the door. Mother opens it.

Mother 'You naughty children! Why did you sleep so long in the forest? We thought you were never coming home.'

Father But their father was pleased to have them back again, for he had been grief-stricken at leaving them all by themselves in the forest.

Mother Not long afterwards, times became very hard again and the famine bit deeply and savagely into their lives.

Hansel One night, when they all lay in bed with empty stomachs, the children heard their mother's ravenous voice again.

Mother 'There's no more food left except half a loaf of bread, and when that's gone that'll be the end of all of us. The children must go, I tell you. Tomorrow first thing, we'll take them even deeper, deeper, right into the belly of the forest so they won't possibly be able to find their way out. It's our only way of saving ourselves.

'You did it before so you'll do it again. You did it before so you'll do it again . . .'

Hansel and **Gretel** 'He did it before, so he'll do it again. He did it before so he'll do it again . . .'

This overlaps, repeats and builds until . . .

Father And in the end, the woodcutter gave in.

Hansel Once more, Hansel waited till his parents fell asleep, and then he got up and tried to get out to collect his pebbles like the last time. But the door had been locked and bolted and Hansel couldn't get out, no matter how hard he tried. He had to go back to bed empty-handed and comfort his little sister.

'No more tears, Gretel. Just try to sleep. I know somehow I'll find something to help us.'

Morning. The family return to the forest, this time with more terror. The movement is silent and slow; almost slow motion.

Hansel Carefully, one tiny crumb at a time, Hansel laid a trail of bread on the path.

In the heart of the forest. A fire is built again.

Mother 'You two sit here and wait, and if you get tired you can go to sleep. Your father and I are going further off to chop wood. And in the evening when we're finished, we'll come and fetch you.'

The children wait and eat and wait and sleep.
Darkness. They wake.

Hansel 'Don't worry, Gretel. When the moon rises, we'll see the breadcrumbs I dropped. They'll show us our way.'

But they didn't find a single breadcrumb, because all the thousands of birds that fly about in the forest had pecked them away and eaten them.

'Don't panic, we'll find our way anyway.'

Gretel But they didn't find it.

Hansel They walked all night and all the following day, and by the next evening they were still hopelessly lost in the bowels of the forest. What's worse, they were hungrier than they had ever been in their skinny young lives.

It was now the third morning since they had left their father. The famished, thirsty children forced themselves to walk again, but they only wandered further and further into the forest, and they knew that unless they found help very soon they would die of hunger.

When it was midday, they saw a beautiful white bird singing on a branch, and the bird's song was so enchanting that Hansel and Gretel stopped to listen to it. As soon as its song was over, the bird flapped its creamy wings and flew off in front of them, and they followed it till it landed on the roof of a little house. When Hansel and Gretel got closer, they saw that the house had bread walls and a roof made of cake and windows made of clear bright sugar.

'Look! This will do us! What wonderful luck! I'll try a slice of the roof, Gretel, and you can start on a window. I bet it'll taste scrumptiously sweet.'

Hansel stretched up and broke off a bit of the roof to see what it tasted like.

Gretel Gretel snapped off a piece of window-pane and nibbled away.

Voice (*Witch, unseen*) Suddenly, they heard a thin little voice calling from inside:
>'Stop your nibbling, little rat,
>It's my house you're gnawing at.'

Hansel and **Gretel** But the chomping children chanted:
>'We're only the wind going past
>Gently blowing on roof and glass.'

Gretel And they just went on munching away.

Hansel Hansel thought the roof was absolutely delicious and pulled off a great big slab of it.

Gretel Gretel bashed out a whole round window-pane and sat down and had a wonderful chewy time.

Witch Then suddenly, the door opened and an old, old woman, bent double on a crutch, came creeping out.

'Well, well, you sweet little things, how did you get here? Come in and stay with me. You'll come to no harm.'

She took the children by the hand and led them into the tempting house. Then she gave them a wonderful meal of creamy milk and mouth-watering pancakes with sugar and chocolate and apples and nuts. After Hansel and Gretel had eaten as much as they could, she made up two soft, comfy little beds with the best white linen, and Hansel and Gretel lay down to sleep.

But the old woman was only pretending to be kind, for she was really a cruel and evil witch who lay in wait for children and had only built her bread house with its cake roof to trap them. When a child fell into her power, she would kill it, cook it and eat it, and that was her favourite feasting-day. Witches have red eyes with which they can't see very far – but they have a powerful sense of smell, as good as an animal's, and they can smell when anyone comes near them. So as Hansel and Gretel had approached her little house in the woods, she'd cackled a spiteful laugh and said:

'Here's two for my belly who won't escape.'

She stands over the sleeping children.

'This will make a tasty morsel for me to swallow.'

She grabs Hansel and forces him into the shed.

(*to Gretel*) 'Get up, you lazy wretch, get water and cook a good meal for your brother. He's locked up outside in the shed and I want him fattened up. When he's nice and plump, I'm going to eat him.'

Gretel Day after day, the best meals were cooked for Hansel, while poor Gretel had to survive on crabshells.

Witch Every morning, the horrible witch groped and fumbled her way out to the shed and shrieked: 'Hansel, stick out your finger for me to feel if you're plump.'

Gretel But clever Hansel held out a little bone instead, and the old crone's red witchy eyes couldn't see it.

12

Witch She thought it was Hansel's finger and was furious and surprised that he went on and on not getting plump. After four weeks of this she lost her patience completely.

'Now then, Gretel. Jump to it and cook him one last meal. Tomorrow, whether he's plump or skinny, fat or lean, I'm going to cut Hansel's throat with my sharpest knife and cook him.'

Hansel and Gretel cry.

'You can cut the bawling. It will do you no good.'

Gretel prepares the oven and cauldron for Hansel's boiling.

'First we'll bake some bread. I've already heated the oven and kneaded the dough. Crawl inside and tell me if it's hot enough for the bread to go in.'

Gretel approaches the oven.

Gretel 'I don't know how to do it. How can I get inside there?'

Witch 'You foolish goose. The opening's big enough for you. I could get into it myself. Look.'

Gretel pushes the Witch into the oven. The Witch burns to death.

Gretel (*opens the shed door*) 'Hansel, we're saved! We're saved! The old witch is dead.'

Hansel And Hansel jumped out, free as a bird released from a cage.

Hansel and **Gretel** And they both danced and cheered and hugged and kissed.

Hansel There was nothing to be afraid of any more, so they went into the witch's house and opened all her cupboards, which were stuffed to bursting with pearls and precious stones.

'These are much better than pebbles.'

He fills his pockets with the jewels.

Gretel 'I'll take some home too.' And she filled her apron full to the brim.

Hansel 'Right. Now let's get out of this witchy forest for good.'

Gretel When the children had walked for a while, they came to the edge of a big, wide river.

Hansel 'I can't see a bridge anywhere. We won't be able to get across.'

Gretel 'And there's no boat either. But look! There's a white duck swimming along. I'm sure it'll help us across if I ask it nicely.' (*Sings:*)

> 'Excuse me, little white duck,
> Gretel and Hansel seem to be stuck.
> A bridge or a boat is what we lack,
> Will you carry us over on your back?'

Sure enough, the duck came swimming and quacking towards them, and Hansel jumped quickly on its back and told Gretel to sit behind him. But sensible Gretel said: 'No. That'll be too heavy for the duck. I think it should take us across one at a time.'

And that is exactly what the kind little duck did. So Hansel and Gretel walked happily on, and the wood became more and more familiar, until at last they saw their father's house in the distance.

Hansel and **Gretel** They began to run, run, run, charged into the kitchen and flung their arms around their father's neck.

Father The poor, unhappy man had not had one happy moment since he had abandoned the children in the forest, and his wife had died and was buried.

Gretel But Gretel shook out the contents of her apron, making the precious stones twinkle and shine upon the floor . . .

Hansel And Hansel threw down handful after handful of white pearls from his pockets.

Hansel and **Gretel** Now it was certain that all their troubles were over, and the grateful woodcutter and Hansel and Gretel lived on together at the edge of the forest and were happy ever after.

THE GOLDEN GOOSE

The Golden Goose is classic farce: those who take themselves seriously are shown to be pompous fools, and the fool wins the hand of the princess. We decided that the story should have a narrator – someone in charge of the proceedings who is also, fleetingly and with great simplicity, the little old man and the trees in the forest. The goose was an arm puppet with false arm and jacket. The magic of the cake and wine is made real through the simplest of tricks. It is a celebration of simple honesty and the joy of laughter. The speech is relaxed and open to the rapport established with an audience.

Narrator Once there was a man who had three sons. Everyone thought that the youngest son was a simpleton. They called him Dummling, and picked on him, sneered at him, and teased him at every opportunity.

One day, the eldest of the three decided to go into the forest and chop wood there. Before he set off, his mother gave him a beautiful, sweet home-made cake and an excellent bottle of wine, in case he needed to eat or drink.

When the eldest son entered the forest, he saw a little grey-haired old man who called out good-day to him and said: 'Please give me a piece of that cake in your pocket, and let me have a gulp of your good wine. I am so hungry and thirsty.'

But the clever son replied coolly:

First Son 'Certainly not. If I give you my cake and wine, I'll have none left for myself and that wouldn't be very smart, would it? Go away.'

Narrator And he turned his back on the little man and strode smartly on. But when he began to chop at his first tree, it was only a few moments before he made a stupid stroke with the axe, and cut himself painfully in the arm. So he had to hurry home and have it bandaged.

And it was the little grey man who had made this happen.

Soon after that, the second son decided to go to the forest; and he, too, received from his mother a delicious cake and a bottle of the best wine.

The little old grey man met him as well, and asked him for a slice of cake and a swig of wine. But the sensible son refused.

Second Son 'That's out of the question. Anything I give to you means less for me and where's the sense in that? On your way.'

Narrator And he left the old man standing there and walked on purposefully. But his punishment came quickly; and as he was hacking away at the tree, he hit himself in the leg so severely that he had to be carried home.

Then Dummling said:

Dummling 'Father, please let me go and cut wood in the forest.'

Narrator His father sighed and tutted:

Father 'Your brothers have hurt themselves already doing that. Be quiet, Dummling. You don't know what you're talking about.'

Narrator But Dummling begged and pleaded for so long that eventually his father said:

Father 'All right then, go! And when you've damaged yourself, perhaps that'll be a lesson to you.'

Narrator Dummling's mother gave him a tasteless cake made with water and baked in the ashes and a bottle of sour beer to wash it down with.

When he arrived in the forest, the little old grey man came up to him and greeted him:

'Give me a bit of your cake and a swallow from your bottle. I am very hungry and thirsty.'

Dummling answered simply and honestly:

Dummling 'I've only got a flour-and-water cake and some stale ale; but if that's good enough for you, you're welcome to share it with me.'

Narrator So they sat down together, and when Dummling took out his cinder-cake it was now a superb sweet cake, and his sour beer had turned into the finest wine.

They ate and drank contentedly, and afterwards the little grey man said: 'Since you have such a kind heart, and share what little you have so generously, I am going to give you the gift of good luck. See that old tree over there? Well, chop it down and you will find something at its roots.' Then the little man left Dummling alone.

Dummling went straight over to the tree and cut it down, and when it fell there was a goose sitting in the roots with feathers of pure gold. He lifted her out, tucked her firmly under his arm, and set off for an inn where he intended to stay the night.

Now, the landlord of the inn had three daughters, and as soon as they saw the goose they were fascinated by it, and curious to find out what wonderful kind of bird it was. And they ended up by longing for one of its golden feathers. The eldest thought:

First Daughter 'I'll be smart and wait for a good opportunity and then I'll pull out one of its feathers for myself.'

Narrator And as soon as Dummling had gone to sleep, she grabbed the goose by its wing. But her fingers and hand stuck to the goose like glue.

Soon afterwards, the second sister came along with exactly the same bright idea of plucking out a golden feather all for herself. But no sooner had she touched her older sister than she was stuck to her.

(*with rag doll*) Then, last of all, the third sister came, determined to take a feather; but the other two screamed out:

First Daughter and **Second Daughter** 'Stay away! For heaven's sake stay away!'

Narrator But she didn't see why she should be the only one to keep away, and thought: 'If they're doing it, why shouldn't I?' . . . and rushed over to them.

Of course, the moment she touched her sister she was stuck to her. And there the three of them had to stay all night, glued to the golden goose.

The next morning, Dummling tucked the goose under his arm and set off into the world; without so much as blinking an eye at the three sisters who were stuck behind him. The silly girls had to run after him, any old way he chose to go; left, right, fast, slow, wherever his legs carried him.

As they were crossing the fields, the Parson noticed them:

Parson 'You ought to be ashamed of yourselves, you disgraceful girls, chasing after a young man through the fields like this. What are young girls coming to?'

Narrator And he seized the youngest by the hand and tried to pull her away. But as soon as his hand touched hers he was stuck fast too, and had to run after them himself until he was red in the face.

Next thing, the Sexton came that way.

Sexton 'Hoy, your reverence, where are you rushing off to? Have you forgotten we've got a christening today?'

Narrator He trotted up to him and tugged at his sleeve, but was stuck to it at once.

While the five of them were jogging like this, one behind

the other, two workers from the fields (*Narrator, plus rag doll*) went past with their hoes. The Parson shouted out to them and begged for their help in setting him and the Sexton free. But no sooner had they touched the Sexton than the two of them became firmly stuck, and now there were seven of them running behind Dummling and his golden goose.

The train sets off – around the stage, through the audience, anywhere the goose wants to take them.

Eventually, they all arrived at a great city.

The King who ruled there had a daughter who was so serious that nothing and no one could make her laugh. Because of this, the King had given his word that whoever could make her laugh could marry her – simple as that.

When Dummling heard about this, he went directly to the King's daughter with his goose and the train of seven people behind him. The solemn-face girl took one look at them all, running up and down as Dummling pleased, and burst out laughing. And she laughed so much it seemed she'd never stop!

Straight away, Dummling asked to marry her, as was his right, and soon enough the peals of laughter became peals of wedding-bells. The wedding was held at once; and Dummling became heir to the kingdom and lived long and happily with his wife.

ASHPUTTEL

Ashputtel was scripted and staged as a piece of dramatic poetry: a fluid movement between the different worlds of the ashes; the tree; and the beauty of the slippers, dresses and feast. The story begins with two blind, crippled beggars – at first their faces are hidden, but they are, of course, the two sisters. At the end we see them as we have at the beginning. We gave the sisters the narration to give Ashputtel an enigmatic power and to emphasize the vicious circle of poetic justice: the sisters tell the story of their own deformation. The Mother Spirit is a figure who, with white gloves, plays the doves and who effects the wonders of the story seen in the twig; the tree; the dressing of Ashputtel; her escapes from, and eventual capture by, the Prince; and finally the terrible blinding of the two sisters. When the sisters narrate a scene they are in they narrate from their perspective – with attitude – otherwise their narration is simple and unobtrusive. Generally the quality of the playing must follow the nature of events and not signal the shock of the violent conclusion. The more delightful the story, the more severe the ending.

Two blind and crippled beggars enter carrying silver slippers and ash. The ash is poured from a large urn, creating Ashputtel's hearth, and the slippers are placed carefully in a prominent place – a story waiting to happen. The following deathbed scene is mimed by the **Father,** *the* **Mother Spirit** *and* **Ashputtel.**

Beggars One dark time, there was a wealthy man whose wife became fatally ill. When she felt that the end of her life was near, she called her only little daughter to her bedside and said:

Younger Beggar 'My darling girl, always try to be good, like you are now, and say your prayers. Then God will look after you, and I will look down at you from heaven and protect you.'

Beggars When she'd said these words, she closed her loving eyes and died. The young girl went out every day to cry beside her mother's grave. When winter came, the snow put down a white shroud on the grave, and when the sun took it off again in the spring, the girl's father remarried.

The two beggars throw off their old grey cloaks – they are young and beautiful.

Elder Sister His new wife brought her two daughters to live with them. Although their faces were as lovely as flowers, their hearts were as ugly as thorns. And so, a time of real unhappiness began for the poor little stepdaughter.

27

Sisters 'Why should this eyesore sit next to us at supper? Those who want to eat bread must earn it. Go to the kitchen, kitchen-maid!'

Elder Sister They stole her pretty dresses and made her wear an old grey smock and forced her perfect feet into wooden clogs.

Sisters 'Ooh, la-di-da! Doesn't the proud princess look elegant today!'

Younger Sister Their bright, mean eyes gleamed, and they laughed at her and put her in the kitchen. She had to do all the hard work from dawn till dusk – get up before sunrise, fetch water, make the fire and do the cooking and washing. As well as this, her stepsisters bullied her and poured peas and lentils into the ashes, then forced her to sit there and pick them all out.

At night, when she was completely worn out and exhausted with work, she was given no bed to sleep in like the others, but had to lie down on the ashes by the hearth. And because this covered her in dust and grime and made her look dirty, they called her:

Sisters 'ASHPUTTEL!'

Elder Sister One day, their father was about to set off to the market-fair and he asked his two stepdaughters what they would like as a present.

'Beautiful dresses.'

Younger Sister 'Pearls and sparkling diamonds.'

Father 'But what about you, Ashputtel? What would you like to have?'

Ashputtel 'Father, break off the first twig that brushes against your hat on the way home and bring it to me.'

Elder Sister So he purchased fine dresses and precious stones for the two stepsisters; and on his way home, as he was riding through a wood, a hazel twig brushed his head and knocked off his hat. So he snapped off the twig and put it in his pocket.

Younger Sister As soon as he arrived back home, he gave his stepdaughters what they had asked for.

Sisters How their eyes widened!

Younger Sister And to Ashputtel he gave the twig from the hazel-bush. Ashputtel said thank you, went out to her mother's grave and planted the twig on it.

Elder Sister She was so unhappy and cried so much that her tears watered the twig as they fell, and it grew into a beautiful tree. Three times every day Ashputtel went to the tree and wept and said her prayers. Each time, a little white bird came and perched on the tree; and whenever Ashputtel wished for something, the bird would drop whatever it was at her feet.

Younger Sister Now, it happened that the King decided that his son must choose a bride; so he announced that a feast would be held.

The Sisters prepare for the feast.

Elder Sister It was to last for three whole days and all the pretty young girls in the country were to be invited.

Younger Sister When the two stepsisters heard that this included them, they were thrilled.

Sisters Their eyes shone and their feet tapped with excitement.

Elder Sister They called Ashputtel and said:

Sisters 'Comb our hair, brush and polish our shoes and

fasten our buckles. We're going to the wedding-feast at the royal palace.'

Elder Sister Ashputtel did as they ordered, but she cried because she wanted to go to the dance as well. She begged her stepmother to let her go, but her stepmother sneered:

Stepmother 'You kitchen tramp! Look at yourself. Do you want to go to the feast all dusty and grimy? You haven't any dresses or shoes, so how do you think you can go dancing, you silly slut?'

Elder Sister But when Ashputtel kept pleading and pleading, she finally said:

Stepmother 'See here. I'll pour two bowls of lentils into the ashes. If you can pick out all the lentils again in one hour then you can come with us to the dance. (*aside*) She'll never manage that, it's impossible.'

Younger Sister Ashputtel went through the back door into the garden and called out:

Ashputtel 'Gentle doves and turtle-doves, all you birds of the sky, come and help me sort out my lentils:
      Into the pot if they're nice to eat,
      But swallow the bad ones with your beak.'

Younger Sister Then two white doves flew in at the kitchen window, and after them came the turtle-doves, and then all the birds of the air came swooping and crowding in and landed on the floor round the ashes.

Elder Sister The doves nodded their small heads and began – peck, peck, pick, pick – and then the other birds joined in – pick, pick, pick, peck, peck, peck – and put all the good lentils into the bowls. They were so quick and efficient that they'd finished within an hour and flown back out of the window.

Younger Sister Ashputtel hurried to show the bowls to her stepmother, bursting with happiness at the thought of going to the wedding-feast. But her stepmother snapped:

Stepmother 'It's no good. You can't come because you haven't any fine dresses, you haven't any shoes, you can't dance and we'd all be ashamed of you.'

Elder Sister And she turned her back on Ashputtel and swept off with her two proud daughters.

Younger Sister When everybody had gone and the house was empty, Ashputtel went to her mother's grave under the hazel-tree and called out:

Ashputtel 'Shake your leaves and branches, little tree,
        Shower gold and silver down on me.'

Elder Sister And the white bird threw down a golden and silver dress and a pair of slippers embroidered in silk and silver.

Quick as a smile, Ashputtel put it all on and hurried to the feast.

She looked so beautiful in the golden dress that her stepsisters and stepmother couldn't see that it was Ashputtel and thought she must be a princess from a foreign land.

Younger Sister The Prince came over to her, bowed deeply, took her hand and danced off with her. He wouldn't let go of her hand, or dance with anyone else; and if another man came up and asked her to dance, he said:

Prince 'She is my partner.'

Elder Sister Ashputtel danced till it was evening, and then she wanted to go home.

Prince 'I shall come with you and escort you home.'

Younger Sister But Ashputtel managed to slip away from him and hid up in the dovecote. The Prince waited until her father came home, and told him that the lovely, mysterious girl had jumped into the dovecote. The father thought:

Father 'Could she possibly be Ashputtel?'

Younger Sister So he sent for the axe and the pick and broke into the dovecote. It was empty.

Sisters When the others came indoors, they saw only grubby little Ashputtel lying among the ashes in her dirty clothes, with a dim little oil-lamp flickering at the fireplace.

Elder Sister Next day, the second day of the feast, when everyone had left, Ashputtel went to the hazel-tree and said:

Ashputtel 'Shake your leaves and branches, little tree,
               Shower gold and silver down on me.'

The bird dresses her in yet more splendid attire. At the feast Ashputtel again dances with the Prince. Once again a man requests her hand for a dance.

Prince 'She is my partner.'

Ashputtel runs from the Prince. For a moment he holds her back. She escapes.

'That strange, unknown girl has escaped me again. I think she must have jumped into your pear-tree.'

Father 'Could it possibly be Ashputtel?'

He chops down the pear-tree. There is no one to be seen.

Elder Sister On the third day:

Ashputtel 'Shake your leaves and branches, little tree,
   Shower gold and silver down on me.'

The bird dresses her in the most splendid attire. At the feast she again dances with the Prince. She is again approached but with a glance the Prince dismisses her admirer. She runs from the Prince again. Her left foot is stuck.

Younger Sister This time, the Prince had thought of a trick.

Elder Sister He had had the whole staircase covered with tar

Younger Sister and as she rushed down it

Elder Sister her left slipper got stuck there.

Sisters The Prince picked it up and looked at it closely. It was small and dainty and golden all over.

Elder Sister The next morning, the Prince took the slipper to the house of Ashputtel's father.

Prince 'I will only marry the girl whose foot fits into this golden shoe.'

Sisters Ashputtel's two stepsisters were thrilled because they had beautiful feet.

Younger Sister The eldest took the shoe up to her bedroom to try on, with her mother watching beside her. But the shoe was too small and she couldn't fit her big toe in. And then her mother handed her a knife and said:

Stepmother 'Slice off your toe. Once you're Queen you won't have to bother with walking.'

The Elder Sister slices off her big toe.

Younger Sister She gritted her teeth against the terrible pain and went back to the Prince. Seeing her foot in the golden slipper, the Prince took her as his bride and rode off with her on his horse. But their way took them past Ashputtel's mother's grave; and there were the two doves perched on the tree calling:

Mother Spirit (*sings:*)
        'Rookity-coo, there's blood in the shoe,
        She chopped her toe, it was too wide,
        She's not your rightful bride.'

Younger Sister The Prince looked at her foot and saw the blood oozing out. He turned round his horse and rode straight back to the house and said she was the wrong girl and that the other sister must try on the shoe.

Elder Sister So the second sister rushed up to her bedroom and managed to squeeze her toes into the shoe, but her heel wouldn't fit.

Stepmother 'Carve a slice off your heel. When you're Queen you won't need to walk anywhere.'

The Younger Sister carves a slice off her heel. The Prince puts her on his horse. They ride off. While passing Ashputtel's mother's grave they hear the doves again.

Mother Spirit (*sings:*)
        'Rookity-coo, there's blood in the shoe,
        She chopped her heel, it was too wide,
        She's not your rightful bride.'

The Prince takes her back to the house.

Prince 'She's not the right one either. Have you got another daughter?'

Father 'No. The only other girl is a grubby little kitchen-maid whom my dead wife left behind her. She can't possibly be the bride.'

34

Prince 'Send for her.'

Stepmother 'No. She's much too dirty. She's not fit to be looked at.'

Elder Sister But the Prince insisted and Ashputtel had to appear.

Ashputtel comes forward. Her foot fits the shoe. Her true identity is revealed.

Prince 'This is my rightful bride!'

Elder Sister The stepmother and the two sisters were thunderstruck and turned ashen-faced with fury

Younger Sister but the Prince put Ashputtel on his horse and rode off with her.

While the Prince and Ashputtel ride past the grave:

Mother Spirit (*sings:*)
'Rookity-coo, a perfect foot in a golden shoe,
Her foot is neither long nor wide,
She is your rightful bride.'

Elder Sister When they had sung this, the two white doves flew down and perched on Ashputtel's shoulders, one on the left and one on the right, and there they stayed.

Sisters On Ashputtel's wedding-day, the two false sisters came, hoping to suck up to her and have a share in her good fortune.

Elder Sister As the bridal procession was entering the church, the eldest sister was on the right

Younger Sister and the younger on the left; and the two doves flew at each of them and pecked out one of her eyes.

Elder Sister And as they were all coming out of the church, the elder sister was on the left

Younger Sister and the younger on the right

Elder Sister and the doves swooped again and pecked out their other eyes.

Sisters And so, because of their cruelty and deceit, they were punished with blindness for the rest of their days.

The Sisters grope and limp to their old grey cloaks. They put them on.

A RIDDLING TALE

A Riddling Tale is dramatized in the lightest possible manner. The flower herself narrates the story and the way the flower is picked gives a visual clue to the answer.

In performance, this tale was given just before the interval. The narrator asked members of the audience to write down their answers to the riddle on pieces of paper, and the first correct answer pulled out of a hat at the end of the performance won a small prize.

The introduction of the riddle and the giving of the answer and prize at the end were improvised. The tone was entirely warm, relaxed, straight, and the occasions were used to announce the interval and to say goodbye. The whole company were on stage for both events.

Narrator Picture this: three women were turned into flowers which grew in a field.

And one of them was allowed to spend each night in her own home.

But once, when her night was nearly over, and the day was coming, forcing her back to the field to be a flower again with her companions, she said to her husband: 'If you will come early this morning and pick me, I shall be set free. I will be able to stay with you for ever.'

So her husband did this.

The riddle of the tale is: How did her husband recognize her when all three flowers were identical?

(For the answer to this riddle, see page 102.)

THE MOUSE, THE BIRD AND
THE SAUSAGE

The Mouse, the Bird and the Sausage is told by one narrator. In the original production he manipulated simple, though finely crafted, puppets around a puppet world. The other performers participated by lighting and sometimes manipulating the puppets.

Narrator Once upon a time, a mouse, a bird and a sausage became friends. They set up house together and lived in perfect peace, happiness and prosperity. It was the bird's job to fly to the forest every day and bring back wood. The mouse had to fetch water, light the fire, and lay the table; the sausage had to do the cooking, and just before dinner-time roll itself once or twice through the broth to give it extra flavour. When the bird came home and put down his load, they sat down at the table, and after a good meal, they slept well till the next morning. It really was a splendid life for them all.

But those who don't appreciate how well off they are are always tempted by something different. One day, the bird met another bird in the forest, and told him all about his excellent circumstances in life. After he'd stopped his boasting, however, the second bird called him a fool to do all the hard work, while the other two obviously had it easy at home.

So the next day, the bird refused to go into the forest. He'd been their slave for long enough, he said, and they weren't going to make a fool of him any longer. It was time to change and arrange things in a different way. The mouse and the sausage pleaded with him; but in spite of all they said, the bird was determined to have his own way. So they drew lots to decide who would do what; and the result was that the sausage was to fetch wood, the mouse was to cook, and the bird was to draw water.

Now look what happened. The sausage went out to the

43

forest for wood, the bird made up the fire, and the mouse put on the broth in the pot. Then the mouse and the bird waited for the sausage to come home with the wood. But the sausage was away for such a long time that they were both worried something had happened; and the bird flew out part of the way to search for it. Not far off, he met a dog who had decided the sausage was rightful prey, grabbed hold of it and eaten it. The bird accused the dog of daylight robbery, but it was all to no good. The dog just said he'd found forged documents on the sausage, so it deserved to die.

The bird sadly picked up the wood and flew home to tell the mouse what had happened. They were both very distressed, but agreed to make the best of things and to stay together. And so the bird laid the table and the mouse prepared the food. She decided she would flavour it by getting into the pot like the sausage used to do; but before she had even reached the middle of the vegetables, she lost her fur and skin and life in the attempt.

When the bird came to carry in their dinner, there was no sign of the cook. In his panic, the bird scattered wood everywhere, calling and searching, but the mouse couldn't be found. Because of the bird's carelessness, a fire had started and he rushed to fetch water to put it out. But the bucket fell into the well, and he fell in after it; and as he could not manage to get out again, he drowned there.

IRON HANS

Iron Hans is a medieval rite of passage – very male, and full of colour, metal, sound and fury. As with Hansel and Gretel, the narration is split between characters and so becomes a part of the action. As the Boy does the most, he speaks to the audience the most and so becomes the central character. The speech has a blunt but not monotonous force: like iron.

First King There was once a King whose castle was next to a great forest which was full of all kinds of wild animals. One day, the King sent out a huntsman to shoot a deer for him; but the huntsman never returned.

'Perhaps he's had an accident,' said the King and sent out two more huntsmen to find him. But they didn't come back either.

So on the third day, the King sent for all his huntsmen and ordered: 'Scour the whole forest, and don't stop searching till you find all three of them.' But none of these huntsmen returned, and not one of the pack of hounds they'd taken with them was ever seen again.

From then on, no one dared to enter the forest. There it stood, dark and silent and empty, with only a solitary eagle or hawk flying over it occasionally.

Huntsman After many years, a huntsman from another country came before the King. He asked to stay at his court and volunteered to enter the dangerous forest.

First King 'The forest is unlucky. You would do no better than all the others, I fear, and you'd never get out.'

Huntsman 'Sir, I will go at my own risk. I am frightened of nothing.'

So the huntsman went into the hushed, gloomy forest with his dog. The dog quickly picked up a scent and followed it; but after running a few yards, it was standing in front of a deep pool and could go no further.

The dog howls, then stiffens. A hand shoots from the pool and pulls her below the surface. Silence.

When the huntsman saw this, he went back and got men to come with buckets to bail the water out of the pool.

When they had scooped deep enough to see the bottom, they discovered a wild man lying there. His body was the colour of rusty iron and his hair hung over his face right down to his knees.

Iron Hans attacks. He is captured.

They tied him up with ropes and pulled him away to the castle.

Everyone there was astonished to see the wild man; but the King had him locked up in an iron cage in the courtyard.

Queen It was forbidden, on pain of death, to open the door, and the Queen herself was to guard the key. From then on, everyone could visit the forest in safety.

The King had a son who was eight years old. One day, the boy was playing in the courtyard with his golden ball, when it bounced into the cage.

Boy 'Can I have my ball back?'

Iron Hans 'No. Not unless you open this door for me.'

Boy 'No, I won't do that. The King has forbidden it.'

Queen The next day he came back and asked for his ball.

Iron Hans 'Open my door.'

Queen But the boy refused. On the third day, the King had ridden out to hunt, and the boy came again and said:

Boy 'I can't open your door even if I wanted to, because I don't have the key.'

Iron Hans 'It's under your mother's pillow; you can get it from there.'

Boy The boy was so anxious to have his ball back that he threw all sense and caution to the winds and fetched the key. The door was difficult to open and he hurt his finger doing it.

Iron Hans steps from the cage and strides away.

The boy was frightened now and ran behind him crying: 'Oh, wild man, don't leave me, or else I shall be beaten!'

Iron Hans The wild man turned round, picked him up, put him on his rusty shoulders and strode quickly into the forest.

Queen When the Queen saw the empty cage she searched for the key, but it had disappeared.

She called for her son, but he did not reply.

She sent her servants to hunt for him in the fields and countryside, but they could not find him.

Everyone could guess what had happened and the whole court was bowed down with grief.

Iron Hans When the wild man was back in the dark forest, he took the boy down from his shoulders and said to him: 'You will not see your mother and father again; but you can stay with me because you freed me, and I feel something for you. If you do everything I tell you to do, you shall get along fine. I have more gold and treasure than anyone else in the world.'

Then he made a bed of moss for the boy to sleep on.

The next morning, the wild man took the boy to a spring and said: 'Look – this golden spring is as bright and clear as crystal. I want you to stay here and make sure nothing falls into it, or it will get polluted. Every evening I'll come back here to see if you have obeyed my instructions.'

Boy The boy sat down beside the spring. Sometimes he saw a golden fish or a golden snake in the water, and he was careful to let nothing fall in.

After a while, his finger began to hurt so much that he dipped it into the water without thinking. He quickly pulled it out again, but saw that it had turned golden all over; and he couldn't wipe it off no matter how hard he tried.

Iron Hans 'What has happened to the spring?'

Boy 'Nothing, nothing.'

Iron Hans 'You have dipped your finger into the water. I'll let it pass this time; but make sure you don't let anything touch the spring again.'

Boy At daybreak next morning, the boy was already sitting by the spring. His finger began to hurt him again. He rubbed it on his head and, by bad luck, a hair floated down into the spring. He pulled it out quickly, but it was completely golden.

Iron Hans 'You have dropped a hair into the spring. I'll let you watch the spring once more, but if it happens a third time then the spring is polluted and you can stay with me no longer.'

Boy On the third morning, the boy sat by the spring and didn't move his finger however badly it hurt him. But the time went very slowly, and he grew bored and began staring at his own reflection in the water. And as he leaned further and further over, trying to stare right into his eyes, his long hair tumbled down from his shoulders into the spring. He pulled himself up quickly, but all the hair on his head was already golden and shone like the sun.

Iron Hans 'You have failed the test and can stay here no more. Go out alone into the world and find out what poverty is like.'

He covers the boy's golden hair with a hood or cap.

'But because you have a good heart, and I mean you well, I will permit you one thing. If you are ever in trouble, come to the forest and shout "Iron Hans!" and I will come and help you. My powers are great – greater than you know – and I have more gold and silver than I need.'

Boy So the boy left the forest, and walked along the highways and byways until at last he arrived at a great city. He looked for work there; but as he had learnt no trade, he could find none. In the end, he went to the palace and asked if they would have him. The courtiers didn't know what job to give him, but they liked him and let him stay. Then the cook employed him, getting him to carry wood and water and sweep out the ashes.

Cook One day, when no one else was available, the cook ordered him to carry the food in to the royal table.

Boy Because he didn't want his golden hair to be seen, the boy kept on his hat.

Second King 'When you serve at the royal table, you must take off your hat.'

Boy 'Oh, sir, I can't. I've got terrible dandruff.'

Second King When he heard this, the King sent for the cook and told him off; asking him what he was thinking of to employ such a boy, and telling him to sack him at once.

Cook But the cook felt sorry for him and swapped him for the gardener's lad.

Gardener So now the boy had to work in the garden, even in bad weather; planting and watering and digging and hoeing.

Boy One summer's day when he was all alone, it was so warm that he took off his hat to get some fresh air on his head.

Princess The sunlight glistened and flashed on his golden hair, and the glittering rays came in through the Princess's window.

'Boy! Bring me a bunch of flowers.'

Boy He quickly pulled on his hat, picked some wild flowers and tied them together.

Gardener 'How can you take the King's daughter such common flowers? Go and find the prettiest and rarest you can for her.'

Boy 'Oh, no. Wild flowers have the strongest perfume. She'll like these best.'

He kneels before the Princess. She takes the flowers from him and smells them. She is pleased.

Princess 'Take off your hat. It's rude to keep it on in my presence.'

Boy 'I can't. I have dandruff on my head.'

The Princess snatches the hat from his head. She stands amazed at his golden hair.

He tried to run out, but the Princess held him by the arm and gave him a handful of sovereigns.

He went away with them, but he didn't care about the

gold. So he took them to the gardener and said: 'Here, these are a present for your children to play with.'

Princess Next day, the Princess again called to him that he was to bring her a bunch of wild flowers.

She tries to snatch his hat from his head. He holds it on.

Boy She gave him another pile of gold coins, but he didn't want to keep them and gave them to the gardener again as toys for his children.

Princess On the third day, things were just the same.

Once again she tries and fails to pull off his hat; she takes flowers and gives gold. She steals a fierce kiss.

Second King Not long after this, the whole country went to war.

The King gathered his troops together, not knowing whether he'd be able to stand up to the enemy army, which was far bigger in numbers than his own.

Boy 'I am grown up now and want to fight in this war too. Give me a horse.'

Laughter.

Boy So the boy went to the edge of the dark forest and called out: 'Iron Hans! . . . Iron Hans! . . . Iron Hans!'

Iron Hans 'What is your request?'

Boy 'I need a fine, strong horse, for I am going to war.'

Iron Hans 'You shall have it, and you shall have even more than you ask for.'

Boy Then the wild man went back into the forest; and it wasn't long before a groom appeared, leading a powerful horse that snorted and pranced and neighed. Behind him, there followed a great troop of warriors, all in armour, their swords flashing in the sun.

The youth mounted the warhorse and rode off at the head of his soldiers.

Second King When he arrived at the battlefield, many of the King's men had already fallen and the rest were close to defeat.

The young man galloped up with his troops of iron, charging here and there among the enemy like thunder and lightning; and he struck down everyone who challenged him.

They began to flee, but he chased them and fought on till there was not one left.

When the King returned to the palace, his daughter came to meet him and congratulated him on winning such a victory.

'It wasn't I who won but a strange knight who came to help me with his own soldiers.'

Princess His daughter wanted to find out who the stranger was.

Second King 'I will announce a great feast. You shall throw a golden apple, and perhaps the stranger will show himself.'

Boy When he heard about the feast, the young man returned to the forest and called Iron Hans.

Iron Hans 'What is your request?'

Boy 'I want to catch the Princess's golden apple.'

Iron Hans 'You practically have it already. You shall also have a suit of red armour and ride on a magnificent chestnut horse.'

Boy When the day of the feast arrived, the young man galloped up to join the other knights, and no one recognized him.

The Second King hands the Princess a golden apple. She steps forward and throws it high. The Boy catches it.

Princess As soon as he'd caught the apple he galloped away.

Knight One of the King's men chased him and managed to pierce his leg with the tip of his sword. His horse reared so violently that his helmet flew from his head.

Astonished, the Knight runs.

Second King They rode back and reported all this to the King.

Princess The next day, the Princess asked the King to summon the gardener's boy.

Second King And he came with his hat still on his head.

The Princess gently takes the hat from the boy's head.

Second King 'Are you the knight who came to the feast and who caught the golden apple?'

Boy 'Yes, and here is the apple. If you need more proof, sir, you can see the wound your men gave me when they chased me. But I am also the knight who helped you to defeat your enemies.'

Second King 'If you can perform such actions, then you are not a gardener's boy. Tell me now, who is your father?'

Boy 'My father is a rich and powerful King, and I have as much gold as I need.'

Second King 'I now see that I have a lot to thank you for. Is there anything I can do to please you?'

Boy 'Yes, there certainly is, sir. Give me your daughter's hand in marriage.'

Princess (*laughs*) 'Well, he doesn't waste his words, does he! But I knew from his golden hair that he wasn't a gardener's boy!'

She goes to him. She touches his hair and slowly kisses him.

Queen His mother came to the wedding and was overjoyed, because she had already given up hope of ever seeing him again.

Boy As they were all sitting at the wedding-feast, the music suddenly stopped, the doors burst open, and a magnificent King entered in great style.

The magnificent King – Iron Hans – goes to the Boy and gives his blessing.

Iron Hans 'I am Iron Hans. I was under a spell that turned me into a wild man – but you have set me free. All my treasure shall be yours.'

THE LADY AND THE LION

The Lady and the Lion has two central characters and is most of all a struggle of love: an extended duet. The Lion Prince guides the first part of the story and so narrates up to his departure as a dove. The Lady then takes over and narrates her patient and remarkable journey. In the original production the voices of the Sun, the Moon, and the Wind were provided by the actor playing the Lion Prince – there was no attempt to disguise this. The story's tone is elegiac, although not tragic. The speech must suggest, but only suggest, the emotional depth of the events.

Lion Prince A merchant was about to go on a long journey, and when he was saying goodbye to his three daughters, he asked each of them what they would like as a present. The eldest asked for:

Eldest Daughter Pearls.

Lion Prince The second asked for:

Second Daughter Diamonds.

Lion Prince But the youngest said:

Lady 'Father, I would like a rose.'

Father 'Even though it's the middle of winter, if I can find one, you shall have it.'

Lion Prince When it was time for him to come home again, he'd found pearls and diamonds for the two eldest; but he had searched everywhere in vain for a rose. This upset him, because his youngest child was his favourite.

He was travelling through a forest. In the middle was a splendid castle and around the castle was a garden.

Half of it was in bright summer time and the other half in gloomy winter. On one side grew the prettiest flowers, but on the other everything was dead and buried in snow.

'What a blessing!' he said to his servant, and ordered him to pick a rose from the beautiful rose-bush there.

But then, as they were riding away, a ferocious lion leapt out.

'Anyone who tries to steal my roses will be eaten by me.'

Father 'I'd no idea it was your garden. Please forgive me. What can I do to save my life?'

Lion Prince 'Nothing can save it. Only if you give me what you first meet when you go home. If you agree to do that, then I'll let you live. *And* you can take the rose for your daughter as well.'

Father 'But it might be my youngest daughter. She loves me best and always runs to meet me when I get home.'

Servant 'It might not be her. It could just as easily be a dog, or a cat.'

Lion Prince So the man gave in, took the rose, and promised that the lion should have whatever he first met when he got home.

When he arrived home and went into his house, his youngest daughter ran up to him and kissed and hugged him. And she was delighted to see that he'd brought her a rose.

Father 'My darling child, this rose has cost too much. In exchange for it, I've promised to give you to a savage lion. When he has you, I'm sure he'll tear you to pieces and eat you.'

Lion Prince He told her everything that had happened and begged her not to go. But she comforted him and said:

Lady 'Dear father, you must keep your promise. I will go there and make the lion gentle, so that I can come safely home to you.'

Lion Prince Next morning, she was shown the road and set off bravely for the forest.

She walks towards the Lion, hesitates for a moment and steps forward with resolution.

Lion Prince The lion, in fact, was an enchanted Prince. By day he and his people were lions; but at night they became humans again.

When she arrived, she was treated kindly and taken to the castle. When night fell, the lion turned into a handsome Prince and welcomed her so courteously that she consented to marry him.

Their wedding was held with much celebration. They lived happily together but he came to her only when it was dusk and left her when morning drew near.

After a while, his deep voice spoke to her from the darkness:

'Your eldest sister is getting married tomorrow and your father is holding a feast. If you would like to go, my lions will escort you there.'

Lady 'Yes, I'd love to see my father again.'

Lion Prince So she set off in the morning with the lions.

There was great joy and happiness when she appeared, because everyone thought she'd been torn to shreds and killed by the wild lion. But she told them her husband was a Prince, and how happy she was. She stayed with them till the feast was over, and then returned to the forest.

When her second sister was getting married, she was invited again, and said to the Prince:

Lady 'I don't want to go alone this time. Come with me.'

Lion Prince But he said it was too dangerous for him, and that he must never be exposed to light. He explained that if, when he was there, even a ray of candlelight fell on him, he would turn into a dove and have to fly about the world for seven long years.

61

Lady 'Oh, do come with me. I will take special care of you and protect you from all light.'

Lion Prince So they set off together.

She chose a room for him there, with walls so thick that no ray of light could get through. The Prince was to lock himself in there when all the candles were lit for the wedding-feast. But there was a tiny crack in the door that nobody noticed.

The wedding was celebrated splendidly; but when the procession came back from church with all its bright, flickering candles, it passed close by his room.

A ray as fine as a single hair fell on the Prince; and as soon as it touched him he was transformed. When she came to find him, there was only a white dove in the room.

'Now for seven years I must fly around the globe. But for every seventh step you take, I will shed one white feather. That will show you the way, and if you follow it you can set me free.'

The dove flew out of the door.

Lady She followed him. And at every seventh step, a little white feather fell down faithfully and showed her the way.

So she walked and walked through the big wild world – never even resting – and the seven years were almost over.

One day, no feather fell; and when she looked up, the dove had disappeared. She thought to herself: 'No one human can help me with this.'

So she climbed up to the sun: 'You shine into every crack, over every mountain; have you seen a white dove flying?'

Sun 'No. I have not. But I'll give you this casket. Open it when you are most in need.'

Lady She thanked the sun and walked on until it was evening.

The moon rose and she asked her: 'You shine all night, over all the fields and the forests; have you seen a white dove flying?'

Moon 'No. I have not. But I'll give you this egg. Break it when you are in great need.'

Lady She thanked the moon and walked on until the night wind began to blow on her. 'You blow on every tree and under every leaf; have you seen a white dove flying?'

Wind 'Yes. I saw the white dove. It has flown to the Red Sea and has become a lion again, because the seven years are now up. The lion is fighting with a dragon, but the dragon is really an enchanted Princess. Follow my advice. Strike the dragon. Then the lion will be able to overpower it and both of them will become human again. When this happens, do not hesitate but set off at once with your beloved Prince and travel home over land and sea.'

The Lady arrives at the Red Sea and sees the Lion fighting the Dragon Princess. He is near defeat. The Lady strikes the Dragon. The Dragon weakens; the Lion overwhelms her. They both become human. The Lady and the Lion Prince are dazzled by the Dragon Princess's beauty.

Dragon Princess When the Princess, who had been the dragon, was released from the spell, she seized the Prince by the arm and carried him off.

Lady The poor girl, who had followed and walked so

far, sat down and wept. But in the end she found her courage and said: 'I will travel as far as the wind blows and as long as the cock crows until I find my love again.'

And she set off along long, long roads until at last she arrived at the castle where the two of them were living together. She discovered soon there was going to be a feast to celebrate their wedding; but she said: 'Heaven will help me.'

Then she opened the casket that the sun had given her. Inside was a dress as dazzling as the sun itself. So she put it on, and went up to the castle.

Everyone stared at her in astonishment, even the bride.

Dragon Princess In fact, the bride liked the dress so much that she wanted it for a wedding-dress and asked if it was for sale.

Lady 'Not for money or land, but for flesh and blood. Let me sleep a night in the same room as the bridegroom.'

Dragon Princess The bride wouldn't agree; but she wanted the dress so badly that at last she said yes. But she told her page to give the Prince a sleeping-draught.

Lady When it was night, and the Prince was already sleeping, she was led into his bedchamber. She sat on the bed and said: 'I have followed after you for seven long years. I have asked the sun and the moon and the night wind for news of you. I have helped you against the dragon. Do you really forget me?'

Lion Prince But the Prince was fast asleep and only thought he heard the wind murmuring and rustling in the trees.

Lady When morning came, she was taken out of his room and had to hand over the golden dress.

She remembered the egg which the moon had given to her. So she cracked it open and out came a clucking hen with twelve little chickens made of gold.

They ran about chirping and cheeping, then crept under their mother's wings. They were the most gorgeous sight anyone could see.

Dragon Princess The tiny chickens delighted the bride so much that she asked if they were for sale.

Lady 'Not for money or land, but for flesh and blood. Let me sleep another night in the bridegroom's chamber.'

Dragon Princess The bride said yes, but she intended to cheat her like before.

Lion Prince But when the Prince was going to bed, he asked the page what the murmuring and rustling in the night had been. Then the page told him everything: that he'd been forced to give him a sleeping-potion, because a strange girl had slept secretly in his room; and that he was supposed to give him another one tonight. The Prince said: 'Pour the sleeping-draught away.'

Lady At night, the girl was led in again; and when she started to tell him all the sad things that had happened and how faithful to him she had been, he immediately recognized the voice of his beloved wife.

Lion Prince 'Now I am really released! I have been in a dream, because the strange princess had bewitched me to make me forget you. But heaven has sent you to me in time, my dear love.'

The Lion Prince and the Lady embrace.

Then they both crept away from the castle, secretly in

the dark, because they were afraid of the strange Princess.

Lady Together they journeyed all the way home. There they lived happily until the end of their days.

THE MAGIC TABLE, THE GOLD-DONKEY
AND THE CUDGEL IN THE SACK

The magic in this story is imagined. The unlimited food on the (real) table is seen in the characters' reaction to it and in their mime. The gold passing out of the Donkey is seen in her shitting-and-spitting. The (real) cudgel is manipulated by the actors, attacking the Landlord and pulling him wherever it wants to take him. Again the characters narrate their own actions. The Magic Table, the Gold-Donkey and the Cudgel in the Sack ends the play because it tells of a small, poor and dull community who gain great and unexpected riches due to hard work and quick wit. Stupidity and folly are forgiven. It is warm and magnificent. The end sequence is a celebration of the imagination – theatre's most magical property.
Throughout the story, contact with the audience should be as great as possible, and the performance should be light and casual.

Father Once there was a tailor who had three sons and one goat.

Goat 'Beh!'

Father The goat provided milk for the four of them; so every day it had to be taken out to graze and fed well.

First Son The three sons took the goat to the churchyard. There was lots of excellent greenery there and they let her graze and jump around.

The goat grazes in the audience: hair, clothes, programmes, etc, serve as grass.

At dusk, when it was time to go home, they asked her:

Sons 'Goat, have you had enough to eat?'

First Son And the goat replied:

Goat 'I've had enough,
        I'm full of the stuff. Beh! Beh!'

Sons 'Let's go home then.'

First Son And they took hold of her halter, led her back to her shed and tied her up safely.

Father 'Well, did you feed the goat properly?'

Sons 'Oh, yes, she's had enough; she's full of the stuff.'

Goat 'Beh! Beh!'

Father But the tailor wanted to check for himself, so he went down to the shed, patted the precious goat, and inquired: 'Goat, are you sure you've had enough to eat?'

The goat replied:

Goat 'There was no grass to eat
Where they took me to feed.
Hard stones on the ground
Were all that I found. Beh! Beh!'

Father (*to his sons*) 'You pack of liars! All three of you
are deceitful and undutiful. Well, you'll not make a fool
out of me any more!'

In his fury, he took his yardstick down from the wall and
thrashed his sons out of the house.

Now the old tailor was all alone with his goat.

'Come along, my little pet, I'll take you out to graze
myself.'

He led her away to a place where there were green
hedges and moist grasses and all the things goats love to
eat.

*Once again the goat grazes in the audience, with even
more devastating affect.*

'Now you can eat your fill for once,' he said; and let her
chomp away till evening.

Then he asked: 'Dear goat, have you had enough to eat?'
And the goat replied:

Goat 'I've had enough,
I'm full of the stuff. Beh! Beh!'

Father 'Come along home then.' And he led her to her
shed and tied her up. As he was leaving, he turned round
and said: 'Now for once I *know* you've really had plenty
to eat.' But the bad goat bleated out:

Goat 'There was no grass to eat
Where you took me to feed.

Hard stones on the ground
Were all that I found. Beh! Beh!'

Father When the tailor heard this, he was horrified and realized how unjustly he'd treated his three sons.

'You ungrateful beast! Just you wait!'

And because the stick would have been too good for it, he fetched his whip and flogged her so badly that she went leaping away for her life.

So the tailor was now all alone in his empty house. He became terribly sad and longed to have his sons back again, but nobody knew where they were.

First Son The eldest boy had become a joiner's apprentice. He was hard-working and conscientious; and when his apprenticeship was over and it was time for him to move on, his master gave him a little table. It was made of wood and looked perfectly ordinary, but there was something special about it.

Joiner 'If you put it before you and say "TABLE, BE LAID!" this splendid little table will immediately cover itself with a clean tablecloth; and there will be a plate with a knife and fork, as many dishes of good hot food as there is room for, and a big, robust, glowing glass of ruby wine to warm the chilliest heart.'

First Son The young man thought to himself: 'Now you've got enough for your whole life,' and he journeyed happily round the world.

Eventually, the boy decided to return home to his father and one evening he came to an inn that was full of guests. They made him welcome and asked him to join them at their meal, otherwise there'd be no food left for him.

'No, I won't take your last few morsels. You shall be my guests instead.'

They thought he was joking with them and they laughed. But he set down his table in the middle of the room and said: 'TABLE, BE LAID!'

He covers the table with a cloth in one smooth gesture – the rest is imagined.

And at once, it was covered with much better food than the landlord of the inn could even dream of, and the delicious smell of it made their noses twitch.

'Help yourselves, my friends,' said the joiner, and they all moved up their chairs, grasped their knives and forks, and tucked in happily.

The amazing thing was that as soon as one dish was empty, another full one took its place immediately.

The guests enjoy the fruits of this marvellous thing.

Landlord The landlord stood watching silently from a corner. 'I could do with a cook like that here at my inn.'

First Son The joiner and his guests ate and drank and laughed and talked late into the night. But finally they went to bed; and the young man lay down to sleep as well, putting his magic table against the wall.

Landlord The landlord's envy kept him awake. He remembered that he had a table which looked exactly the same up in his attic. So very quietly he fetched it, crept in, and swapped it for the magic table.

He does this. The old table is mimed. The magic table is denied its magic as soon as he takes the tablecloth from it.

First Son Next morning, the joiner paid his bill, lifted the table on to his back – never dreaming that it was the wrong one – and set off for his father's house. He arrived home at midday and his father was overjoyed to see him.

Father 'Well, well, well, my dear boy. What have you learnt?'

First Son 'Father, I've become a joiner.'

Father 'That's a worthwhile trade, and what have you brought back from your travels?'

First Son 'Father, I've brought the most wonderful thing – a little table.'

Father 'Well, you've made no work of art here. It's just a shabby old table.'

First Son 'But it's a magic table. Just ask all our friends and relatives over and we'll give them a real treat. They can eat and drink as much as they want.'

So when all the guests had assembled, he put his little table in the middle of the room and said: 'TABLE, BE LAID!'

But this table did nothing. It stayed just as bare and wooden and still as any other table that doesn't understand when it's spoken to.

Then the poor joiner realized what had happened at the inn; and he stood there ashamed and embarrassed that everyone would think he was a liar. His relations had to go home with empty stomachs.

His father got out some cloth and went on tailoring, and the joiner went to join a master joiner.

Second Son The second son had fetched up at a mill and apprenticed himself to the miller. When he'd finished his time, his master said:

Miller 'Because you've been such a good worker, I'm

going to give you a donkey. He's very special. He doesn't pull a cart and he won't carry sacks of flour either.'

Second Son 'Then what's the use of him?'

Miller 'He spits out gold. If you stand him on a cloth and say "SHITSY-SPITSY!" this magnificent creature will produce gold coins for you from both ends!'

Second Son 'This is wonderful,' said the young man. And he thanked his master and set off into the world.

After travelling for a time, he decided to visit his father. On his way home, he stopped at the same inn as his brother. He was leading his donkey, and the landlord was about to take it for him, when he said: 'Don't bother yourself, landlord. I'll take my donkey to the stable myself.'

He takes the cloth from the magic table.

Landlord But he took the tablecloth with him. The landlord couldn't understand this at all, so he secretly followed the boy. He crept along and discovered that his guest had bolted the stable door. Filled with curiosity he peered in through a gap in the wood.

Second Son 'SHITSY-SPITSY!'

The donkey begins to produce gold.

Landlord Suddenly the beast began to throw out gold from both ends – showers and showers of it.

'Well, who would believe it. That's a quick way to make gold. I could use a moneybag like that.'

The landlord sneaked down to the stables overnight, led the gold-donkey away and tied up another donkey in its place.

Second Son Early next morning, the boy set off. He

74

arrived home at midday and his father gave him a warm welcome.

Father 'Well, well, well, my boy, and what have you become?'

Second Son 'I am a miller, father.'

Father 'And what have you brought back with you from your travels?'

Second Son 'Just a donkey.'

Father 'We're all right for donkeys around here. We could have done with a decent goat.'

Second Son 'But this is no ordinary donkey, father, it's a gold-donkey. Ask all our friends and relatives round and I'll make every one of them rich.'

Father 'That'll do me. I won't need to work my old fingers to the bone with this needle any more.'

The relatives arrive.

Second Son 'Watch this everybody!'

'SHITSY-SPITSY!'

But what landed on the cloth was certainly not gold, and it was obvious that this donkey could produce no more than any other old donkey.

The poor young miller was mortified. So the old man had to take up his needle again and the boy had to get a job with a miller.

Third Son The youngest son had apprenticed himself to a turner, and because this is such a skilled trade, he took longest to learn it.

His brothers wrote him a letter, telling him of their bad luck and how the villainous landlord had stolen their magic gifts on the night before they got home.

75

When the young turner had completed his time and was setting out to travel, his master rewarded him for his fine, honest work with a sack.

Turner 'It's got a cudgel inside.'

Third Son 'Well, I can sling the sack over my shoulder and make good use of it, but the cudgel will just make it heavy to carry. What use is it?'

Turner 'Plenty use. If anyone ever does you any harm at all, just say "CUDGEL, OUT OF THE SACK!" and the cudgel will jump out at whoever's there and dance so madly on their backs that they won't be able to walk for a week. And it won't stop till you say "CUDGEL, BACK IN THE SACK!" '

Third Son The young miller said thank you, and slung the sack over his shoulder.

Eventually, the boy arrived at the bad landlord's inn. He put his sack down in front of him on the table, and started to talk about all the miraculous things he'd seen on his travels.

'Oh yes, you come across magic tables and gold-donkeys and all that sort of thing – excellent in their way and I've nothing against them – but they're nothing compared to the treasure I've got in my sack here.'

Landlord The landlord listened excitedly and wondered what it could be. He thought: 'Perhaps his sack is filled with jewels. If it is, *I* should have them as well. Twice is nice, but thrice is nicer.'

At bedtime, his guest lay down on the bench and put his sack under his head for a pillow. When the landlord thought he was sound asleep, he sneaked up and began tugging very gently and slowly at the sack.

Third Son 'CUDGEL, OUT OF THE SACK!'

The cudgel beats the Landlord (and the audience) until he can take no more.

'Unless you give back the magic table and the gold-donkey, the painful dance will begin again.'

Landlord 'Oh no, I'll give you the lot, sir, honestly – just tell that hideous thing to get back in its sack.'

Third Son 'Very well, I shall give you mercy as well as justice, but just you mind your step in future.

'CUDGEL, BACK IN THE SACK!'

And the cudgel had a rest.

Next morning, the turner went home to his father with the magic table and the gold-donkey. His father was delighted to see him, and asked him what he had learnt.

'I am a turner, dear father.'

Father 'A very skilful trade. And what have you brought home from your travels?'

Third Son 'Something very valuable, father. A cudgel in a sack.'

Father 'A cudgel? What for? You can hack one off the nearest tree.'

Third Son 'Not one like this, dear father. Send for my brothers and invite all our friends and relations. I'll fill their bellies with food and drink and their pockets with gold.'

When they were all together, the turner put a cloth down on the floor, led in the gold-donkey, and said to his brother: 'Now my dear brother, speak to your donkey!'

Second Son 'SHITSY-SPITSY!'

The donkey rains gold coins to the relatives' unbridled delight.

77

And there and then it began to rain gold coins on the cloth. The donkey didn't stop till everyone's pockets were bulging.

Third Son Then the turner fetched the little table and said: 'Speak to your table, my good brother.'

First Son 'TABLE, BE LAID!'

And the table was crowded with every delicious dish and the best wine. Then they had a feast the like of which had never been known in the poor tailor's house, and the whole family stayed together till late at night, having the most wonderful party.

They share the food with the audience.

Father The tailor locked away his needle and thread and yardstick, and lived long and happy and prosperous with his three fine sons.

Grimm Tales

adapted by Carol Ann Duffy

Hansel and Gretel

It was no more than once upon a time when a poor woodcutter lived in a small house at the edge of a huge, dark forest. Now, the woodcutter lived with his wife and his two young children – a boy called Hansel and a little girl called Gretel. It was hard enough for him to feed them all at the best of times – but these were the worst of times; times of famine and hunger and starvation; and the woodcutter was lucky if he could get his hands on even a simple loaf of bread. Night after hungry night, he lay in his bed next to his thin wife, and he worried so much that he tossed and he turned and he sighed and he mumbled and he moaned and he just couldn't sleep at all. 'Wife, wife, wife,' he said to Hansel's and Gretel's stepmother. 'What are we going to do? How can we feed our two poor children when we've hardly enough for ourselves? Wife, wife, what can be done?' And as he fretted and sweated in the darkness, back came the bony voice of his wife; a voice as fierce as a famine. 'Listen to me, husband,' she said. 'Tomorrow at first light we'll take the children into the forest, right into the cold, black heart of it. We'll make a fire for them there and give them each one last morsel of bread. Then we'll pretend to go off to our work and we'll leave them there all by themselves. They'll never be able to find their way back home on their own. We'll be rid of them for good and only have to worry about feeding ourselves.' But when the woodcutter heard these hard, desperate words he said no. 'No, no, wife, I can't do that. How could I have the heart to leave young Hansel and Gretel in the forest? The wild beasts would soon sniff them out and eat them alive.' But his wife was determined. 'You fool,' she said with tight lips, 'do you want all four of us to starve to death? You might as well start smoothing the wood for our coffins.' And she gave the poor, heartsore woodcutter no peace until he agreed to do as she said. 'But I feel so sorry for my helpless little children,' he wept. 'I can't help it.'

Now, Hansel and Gretel had been so hungry that night that they hadn't been able to sleep either, and they'd heard every cruel word of their stepmother's terrible plan. Gretel cried bitter, salt tears, and said to Hansel: 'Now we're finished.' But Hansel comforted her. 'Don't cry, Gretel. Don't be sad. I'll think of a way to save us.' And when their father and stepmother had finally gone to sleep, Hansel got up, put on his coat, opened the back door, and crept out into the midnight hour. There was bright, sparkling moonlight outside and the white pebbles on the ground shone like silver coins and precious jewels. Hansel bent down and filled his empty pockets with as many pebbles as he could carry. Then he went back inside and said to Gretel: 'Don't worry, Gretel, you can go to sleep now. We'll be fine, I promise.' And he got back into bed.

At dawn, before the sun had properly risen, their stepmother came and woke the two children. 'Get up, you lazy scraps, we're going into the forest to chop wood.' Then she gave each of them a miserable mouthful of bread: 'There's your lunch; think yourselves lucky, and don't eat it all at once, because there's nothing else.' Gretel put the bread in her apron pocket, because Hansel's pockets were crammed with pebbles. Then the whole family set off along the path to the forest. Hansel kept stopping and looking back towards the house, until finally the woodcutter called to him: 'Hansel, what are you trailing behind for and looking at? Keep up with the rest of us.' 'Sorry, father,' said Hansel, 'I'm just looking back at my white kitten. It's sitting up there on our roof, saying goodbye.' 'You stupid boy,' said his stepmother. 'That's not your kitten. It's just the light of the morning sun glinting on the chimney. Now come on.'

But, of course, Hansel hadn't been looking at anything at all. He'd been throwing the white pebbles from his pocket on to the path.

The forest was immense and gloomy. When they had reached the middle, the woodcutter said: 'Now Hansel, now Gretel, gather up some wood and I'll make a nice fire to keep you warm.' Hansel and Gretel collected a big pile of firewood and when it was set alight and the flames were like burning tongues, their stepmother said: 'Now lie down by the fire and rest. We're going further into the forest to chop wood. When we're finished working, we'll come back and get you.' The children sat by the fire, and when midday came, they chewed on their small portions of bread. They could hear the blows of a woodcutter's axe nearby and they thought that their father was close. But it wasn't an axe, it was just a branch that he had tied to an old, withered tree and the wind was blowing it to and fro, to and fro. After they had waited and waited and waited, the children's eyes grew as heavy as worry and they fell fast asleep.

When at last they woke up, it was already pitch dark, darker than a nightmare. Gretel began to cry and said: 'How are we going to find our way out of this enormous forest?' But Hansel tried to cheer her up. 'Just wait a bit till the moon rises, Gretel, then we'll find our way home all right.' And when the moon had risen, casting its brilliant, magical light, Hansel took his little sister by the hand and followed the pebbles. They shone like newly minted coins, like cats' eyes, like diamonds, and showed them the way. They walked all through the night, and at daybreak they knocked on the door of their father's house. When their stepmother opened it and saw it was Hansel and Gretel, she said: 'You naughty children! Why did you sleep so long in the forest? We thought you were never coming home.' But their father was pleased to have them back again, for he had been grief-stricken at leaving them all by themselves in the forest.

Not long afterwards, times became very hard again and the famine bit deeply and savagely into their lives. One night, when they all lay in bed with empty stomachs, the children heard their stepmother's ravenous voice again: 'There's no more food left except half a loaf of bread, and when that's gone that'll be the end of all of us. The children must go, I tell you. Tomorrow first thing, we'll take them even deeper, deeper, right into the belly of the forest so they won't possibly be able to find their way out. It's our only way of saving ourselves.' Although the woodcutter grew very upset and thought that it was better to share your last crumb with your children, his wife wouldn't listen to a word he said. Her sharp voice pecked on and on at him: 'You did it before so you'll do it again. You did it before so you'll do it again.' And in the end, the poor starving woodcutter gave in.

Once more, Hansel waited till his parents fell asleep, and then he got up and tried to get out to collect his pebbles like the last time. But the stepmother had locked and bolted the door and Hansel couldn't get out, no matter how hard he tried. He had to go back to bed empty-handed and comfort his little sister. 'No more tears, Gretel,' he said. 'Just try to sleep. I know somehow I'll find something to help us.'

It was very, very early when their stepmother came and shook the children out of bed. She gave them each a piece of bread, but they were even smaller pieces than before. On the way to the forest, Hansel crumbled his bit of bread in his pocket, and kept pausing to throw a crumb on the ground. 'Hansel, why do you keep stopping and looking behind you?' said the woodcutter. 'Get a move on.' 'I'm only looking back at my little dove, father,' said Hansel. 'It's sitting on our roof trying to say goodbye to me.' 'You idiotic boy,' snapped his stepmother, 'that isn't your dove. It's the sun shining on the chimney-pot.' But carefully, one tiny crumb at a time, Hansel laid a trail of bread on the path.

84

And now the stepmother had led the children right into the deepest, densest part of the forest, to where they had never been in their whole lives. A big, licking fire was lit again and she told them: 'You two sit here and wait, and if you get tired you can go to sleep. Your father and I are going further off to chop wood. And in the evening when we're finished, we'll come and fetch you.'

After a while, Gretel shared her miserly lump of bread with Hansel, who had scattered his piece on the path. Then they fell asleep, and the long evening passed, but nobody came to take them home. The night grew darker and darker, and when they woke up, it was too black to see a thing. 'Don't worry, Gretel,' said Hansel. 'When the moon rises, we'll see the breadcrumbs I dropped. They'll show us our way.' As soon as the full moon came, glowing and luminous, the two children set off.

But they didn't find a single breadcrumb, because all the thousands of birds that fly about in the forest had pecked them away and eaten them. Hansel said to Gretel: 'Don't panic, we'll find our way anyway.' But they didn't find it. They walked all night and all the following day, and by the next evening they were still hopelessly lost in the bowels of the forest. What's worse, they were hungrier than they had ever been in their skinny young lives, because they had nothing to eat except for a few berries they'd managed to find. Eventually, Hansel and Gretel were so weak and exhausted that their legs wouldn't carry them one step further. So they lay down under a tree and fell fast asleep.

It was now the third morning since they had left their father. The famished, thirsty children forced themselves to walk again, but they only wandered further and further into the forest, and they knew that unless they found help very soon they would die of hunger. When it was midday, they saw a beautiful white bird singing on a branch, and the bird's song was so enchanting that Hansel and Gretel stopped to listen to it. As soon as its song was over, the bird flapped its creamy wings and flew off in front of them, and they followed it till it landed on the roof of a little house. When Hansel and Gretel got closer, they saw that the house had bread walls and a roof made of cake and windows made of clear bright sugar. 'Look!' cried Hansel. 'This will do us! What wonderful luck! I'll try a slice of the roof, Gretel, and you can start on a window. I bet it'll taste scrumptiously sweet.' Hansel stretched up and broke off a bit of the roof to see what it tasted like, and Gretel snapped off a piece of window-pane and nibbled away. Suddenly, they heard a thin little voice calling from inside:

> 'Stop your nibbling, little rat,
> It's my house you're gnawing at.'

But the chomping children chanted:

> 'We're only the wind going past,
> Gently blowing on roof and glass.'

And they just went on munching away. Hansel thought the roof was absolutely delicious and pulled off a great slab of it. Gretel bashed out a whole round window-pane and sat down and had a wonderful chewy time. Then suddenly, the door opened and an old, old woman, bent double on a crutch, came creeping out. Hansel was so scared and Gretel was so frightened that they both dropped what they were holding. But the old woman wagged her wizened head and said: 'Well, well, you sweet little things, how did you get here? Come in and stay with me. You'll come to no harm.' She took the children by the hand and led them into the tempting house. Then she gave them a wonderful meal of creamy milk and mouth-watering pancakes with sugar and chocolate and apples and nuts. After Hansel and Gretel had eaten as much as they could, she made up two soft, comfy little beds with the best white linen, and Hansel and Gretel lay down to sleep.

But the old woman was only pretending to be kind, for

she was really a cruel and evil witch who lay in wait for children and had only built her bread house with its cake roof to trap them. When a child fell into her power, she would kill it, cook it and eat it, and that was her favourite feasting-day. Witches have red eyes which they can't see very far with – but they have a powerful sense of smell, as good as an animal's, and they can smell when anyone comes near them. So as Hansel and Gretel had approached her little house in the woods, she'd cackled a spiteful laugh and said nastily: 'Here's two for my belly who shan't escape.'

Early next morning before the children had woken, she was already standing by their beds looking greedily down at them. They looked so sweet lying there with their rosy cheeks that she muttered to herself: 'This will make a tasty morsel for me to swallow.' Then she seized Hansel with her long claws and dragged him off to a little shed outside and locked him up behind the door with iron bars. Hansel screamed his head off, but it was no use. Then the witch went to Gretel and shook her awake and shouted: 'Get up, you lazy wretch, get water and cook a good meal for your brother. He's locked up outside in the shed and I want him fattened up. When he's nice and plump, I'm going to eat him.' Gretel started to cry hot, stinging tears, but it was no good, and she had to do what the wicked witch told her.

Day after day, the best meals were cooked for Hansel, while poor Gretel had to survive on crabshells. Every morning, the horrible witch groped and fumbled her way out to the shed and shrieked: 'Hansel, stick out your finger for me to feel if you're plump.' But clever Hansel held out a little bone instead, and the old crone's red witchy eyes couldn't see it. She thought it was Hansel's finger and was furious and surprised that he went on and on not getting plump. After four weeks of this, she lost her patience completely and refused to wait a day longer. 'Now then, Gretel,' she shouted. 'Jump to it and cook him one last meal. Tomorrow, whether he's plump or skinny, fat or

87

lean, I'm going to cut Hansel's throat with my sharpest knife and cook him.' Gretel sobbed and wailed as the witch forced her to carry the water for cooking, and her face was soaked with tears. 'Who can help us now?' she cried. 'If only the wild beasts had eaten us in the forest, then at least we'd have died together.' 'You can cut that bawling out,' said the witch. 'It won't do you any good.'

Next morning, Gretel had to go out and hang up a big cooking-pot of water and light the fire. 'First we'll bake some bread,' said the witch. 'I've already heated the oven and kneaded the dough.' She pushed and pinched poor Gretel over to where the oven was, with keen flames leaping out of it already. 'Crawl inside and tell me if it's hot enough for the bread to go in.' And the witch's dreadful, gluttonous plan was to shut the oven door once Gretel was inside, so she could roast her and eat her too. But Gretel guessed this, and said: 'I don't know how to do it. How can I get inside there?' 'You foolish goose,' snapped the witch. 'The opening's big enough for you. I could get into it myself. Look.' And the witch hobbled up and poked her ugly head inside the oven. Then Gretel gave her such a push, such a big shove, that she fell right into the middle of the oven. Gretel slammed the iron door shut with shaking hands and bolted it. The witch began to shriek and howl in the most frightful way; but Gretel ran outside and the heartless witch burnt agonizingly to death.

Gretel ran straight to Hansel's shed and opened it, shouting: 'Hansel, we're saved! We're saved! The old witch is dead.' And Hansel jumped out, free as a bird released from a cage, and they both danced and cheered and hugged and kissed. There was nothing to be afraid of any more, so they went into the witch's house and opened all her cupboards, which were stuffed to bursting with pearls and precious stones. 'These are much better than pebbles,' said Hansel. He crammed his pockets with as much as he could, and Gretel said: 'I'll take some home too,' and filled her apron full to the brim. 'Right,' said Hansel. 'Now let's go and get out of this witchy forest for good.'

When the children had walked for a while, they came to the edge of a big, wide river. 'I can't see a bridge anywhere,' said Hansel. 'We won't be able to get across.' 'And there's no boat either,' said Gretel. 'But look! There's a white duck swimming along. I'm sure it'll help us across if I ask it nicely.' So she called out:

'Excuse me, little white duck,
Gretel and Hansel seem to be stuck.
A bridge or a boat is what we lack,
Will you carry us over on your back?'

Sure enough, the duck came swimming and quacking towards them, and Hansel jumped quickly on its back and told Gretel to sit behind him. But sensible Gretel said: 'No. That'll be too heavy for the duck. I think it should take us across one at a time.' And that is exactly what the kind little duck did. So Hansel and Gretel walked happily on, and the wood became more and more familiar, until at last they saw their father's house in the distance. They began to run, run, run, charged into the kitchen and flung their arms around their father's neck. The poor, unhappy man had not had one happy moment since he had abandoned the children in the forest, and his wife had died and was buried. But Gretel shook out the contents of her apron, making the precious stones twinkle and shine upon the floor, and young Hansel threw down handful after handful of white pearls from his pockets. Now it was certain that all their troubles were over, and the grateful woodcutter and Hansel and Gretel lived on together at the edge of the forest and were happy ever after.

So that was that. Look! There goes a rat! Who'll catch it and skin it and make a new hat?

The Golden Goose

Once there was a man who had three sons. Everyone thought that the youngest son was a simpleton. They called him Dummling, and picked on him, sneered at him, and teased him at every opportunity. One day, the eldest of the three decided to go into the forest and chop wood there. Before he set off, his mother gave him a beautiful, sweet home-made cake and an excellent bottle of wine, in case he needed to eat or drink. When the eldest son entered the forest, he saw a little grey-haired old man who called out good-day to him and said: 'Please give me a piece of that cake in your pocket, and let me have a gulp of your good wine. I am so hungry and thirsty.' But the clever son replied coolly: 'Certainly not. If I give you my cake and wine, I'll have none left for myself and that wouldn't be very smart, would it? Go away.' And he turned his back on the little man and strode smartly on. But when he began to chop at his first tree, it was only a few moments before he made a stupid stroke with the axe, and cut himself painfully in the arm. So he had to hurry home and have it bandaged. And it was the little grey man who had made this happen.

Soon after that, the second son decided to go to the forest; and he, too, received from his mother a delicious cake and a bottle of the best wine. The little old grey man met him as well, and asked him for a slice of cake and a swig of wine. But the sensible son refused. 'That's out of the question. Anything I give to you means less for me and where's the sense in that? On your way.' And he left the old man standing there and walked on purposefully. But his punishment came quickly; and as he was hacking away at the tree, he hit himself in the leg so severely that he had to be carried home.

Then Dummling said: 'Father, please let me go and cut wood in the forest.' His father sighed and tutted: 'Your brothers have hurt themselves already doing that. Be quiet, Dummling. You don't know what you're talking about.' But Dummling begged and pleaded for so long that eventually his father said: 'All right then, go! And when you've damaged yourself, perhaps that'll be a lesson to you.' Dummling's mother gave him a tasteless cake made with water and baked in the ashes and a bottle of sour beer to wash it down with. When he arrived in the forest, the little old grey man came up to him and greeted him: 'Give me a bit of your cake and a swallow from your bottle. I am very hungry and thirsty.' Dummling answered simply and honestly: 'I've only got a flour-and-water cake and some stale ale; but if that's good enough for you, you're welcome to share it with me.' So they sat down together, and when Dummling took out his cinder-cake it was now a superb sweet cake, and his sour beer had turned into the finest wine. They ate and drank contentedly, and afterwards the little grey man said: 'Since you have such a kind heart, and share what little you have so generously, I am going to give you the gift of good luck. See that old tree over there? Well, chop it down and you will find something at its roots.' Then the little man left Dummling alone. Dummling went straight over to the tree and cut it down, and when it fell there was a goose sitting in the roots with feathers of pure gold. He lifted her out, tucked her firmly under his arm, and set off for an inn where he intended to stay the night.

Now, the landlord of the inn had three daughters, and as soon as they saw the goose they were fascinated by it, and curious to find out what wonderful kind of bird it was. And they ended up by longing for one of its golden feathers. The eldest thought: 'I'll be smart and wait for a good opportunity and then I'll pull out one of its feathers for myself.'

And as soon as Dummling had gone out, she grabbed the goose by its wing. But her fingers and hand stuck to the goose like glue. Soon afterwards, the second sister came along with exactly the same bright idea of plucking out a golden feather all for herself. But no sooner had she touched her older sister than she was stuck to her. Then, last of all, the third sister came, determined to take a feather; but the other two screamed out: 'Stay away! For heaven's sake stay away!' But she didn't see why she should be the only one to keep away, and thought: 'If they're doing it, why shouldn't I?' and rushed over to them. Of course, the moment she'd touched her sister she was stuck to her. And there the three of them had to stay all night, glued to the golden goose.

The next morning, Dummling tucked the goose under his arm and set off into the world; without so much as blinking an eye at the three sisters who were stuck behind him. The silly girls had to run after him, any old way he chose to go; left, right, fast, slow, wherever his legs carried him. As they were crossing the fields, the Parson noticed them, and when he saw the procession following Dummling, he said sternly: 'You ought to be ashamed of yourselves, you disgraceful girls, chasing after a young man through the fields like this. What are young girls coming to?' And at the same time, he seized the youngest by the hand and tried to pull her away. But as soon as his hand touched hers he was stuck fast too, and had to run after them himself till he was red in the face. Next thing, the Sexton came that way, and seeing the highly respectable Parson, that pillar of the community, running after three girls, he was very shocked indeed and called out: 'Hoy, your reverence, where are you rushing off to? Have you forgotten we've got a christening today?' He trotted up to him and tugged at his sleeve, but was stuck to it at once. While the five of them were jogging like this, one behind the other, two workers from the fields went past with their hoes. The Parson shouted out to them and begged for their help in setting him and the Sexton free. But no sooner had they touched the Sexton than the two of them became firmly stuck, and now there were seven of them running behind Dummling and his golden goose.

Eventually, they all arrived at a city. The King who ruled there had a daughter who was so serious that nothing and no one could make her laugh. Because of this, the King had given his word that whoever could make her laugh could marry her – simple as that. When Dummling heard about this, he went directly to the King's daughter with his goose and the train of seven people behind him. The solemn-faced girl took one look at them all, running up and down as Dummling pleased, and burst out laughing. And she laughed so much it seemed she'd never stop! Straight away, Dummling asked to marry her, as was his right, and soon enough the peals of laughter became peals of wedding-bells. The wedding was held at once; and Dummling became heir to the kingdom and lived long and happily with his wife.

Ashputtel

One dark time, there was a wealthy man whose wife became fatally ill. When she felt that the end of her life was near, she called her only little daughter to her bedside and said: 'My darling girl, always try to be good, like you are now, and say your prayers. Then God will look after you, and I will look down at you from heaven and protect you.' When she'd said these words, she closed her loving eyes and died. The young girl went out every day to cry beside her mother's grave. When winter came, the snow put down a white shroud on the grave, and when the sun took it off again in the spring, the girl's father remarried.

His new wife brought her two daughters to live with them. Although their faces were as lovely as flowers, their hearts were as ugly as thorns. And so, a time of real unhappiness began for the poor little stepdaughter. 'Why should this eyesore sit next to us at supper?' they squawked. 'Those who want to eat bread must earn it. Go to the kitchen, kitchen-maid!' They stole her pretty dresses and made her wear an old grey smock and forced her perfect feet into wooden clogs. 'Ooh, la-di-da!' they sniggered. 'Doesn't the proud princess look elegant today!' Their bright, mean eyes gleamed, and they laughed at her and put her in the kitchen. She had to do all the hard work from dawn till dusk – get up before sunrise, fetch water, make the fire and do the cooking and washing. As well as this, her stepsisters bullied her and poured peas and lentils into the ashes, then forced her to sit there and pick them all out. At night, when she was completely worn out and exhausted with work, she was given no bed to sleep in like the others, but had to lie down on the ashes by the hearth. And because this covered her in dust and grime and made her look dirty, they called her 'Ashputtel'.

One day, their father was about to set off to the market-fair and he asked his two stepdaughters what they would like as a present. 'Beautiful dresses,' said one. 'Pearls and sparkling diamonds,' said the second. 'But what about you, Ashputtel?' he said. 'What would you like to have?' 'Father, break off the first twig that brushes against your hat on the way home and bring it to me.' So he purchased fine dresses and precious stones for the two stepsisters; and on his way home, as he was riding through a wood, a hazel twig brushed his head and knocked off his hat. So he snapped off the twig and put it in his pocket. As soon as he arrived back home, he gave his stepdaughters what they had asked for – how their eyes widened! – and to Ashputtel he gave the twig from the hazel-bush. Ashputtel said thank you, went out to her mother's grave and planted the twig on it. She was so unhappy and cried so much that her tears watered the twig as they fell, and it grew into a beautiful tree. Three times every day Ashputtel went to the tree and wept and said her prayers. Each time, a little white bird came and perched on the tree; and whenever Ashputtel wished for something, the bird would drop whatever it was at her feet.

Now, it happened that the King decided that his son must choose a bride; so he announced that a feast would be held. It was to last for three whole days and all the pretty young girls in the country were to be invited. When the two stepsisters heard that this included them, they were thrilled, and their eyes shone and their feet tapped with excitement. They called Ashputtel and said: 'Comb our hair, brush and polish our shoes and fasten our buckles. We're going to the wedding-feast at the royal palace.' Ashputtel did as they ordered, but she cried because she wanted to go to the dance as well. She begged her stepmother to let her go, but her stepmother sneered: 'You kitchen tramp! Look at yourself. Do you want to go to the feast all dusty and grimy? You haven't any dresses or shoes, so how do you think you can go dancing, you silly slut?' But when Ashputtel kept pleading and pleading, she finally said: 'See here. I've poured this bowl of lentils into the ashes. If you can pick out all the lentils again in two hours, then you can come with us to the dance.'

Ashputtel went through the back door into the garden and called out: 'Gentle doves and turtle-doves, all you birds of the sky come and help me sort out my lentils:

> Into the pot if they're nice to eat,
> But swallow the bad ones with your beak.'

Then two white doves flew in at the kitchen window, and after them came the turtle-doves, and then all the birds of the air came swooping and crowding in and landed on the floor round the ashes. The doves nodded their small heads and began – peck, peck, pick, pick – and then the other birds joined in – pick, pick, pick, peck, peck, peck – and put all the good lentils into the bowl. They were so quick and efficient that they'd finished within an hour and flown back out of the window. Ashputtel hurried to show the bowl to her stepmother, bursting with happiness at the thought of going to the wedding-feast. But her stepmother said: 'No, Ashputtel, you've got no dress and you can't dance. They'll only laugh at you.' But when Ashputtel burst into tears, she said: 'If you can sort out two bowlfuls of lentils out of the ashes in one hour, you can come with us. She'll never manage that,' thought the stepmother to herself as she poured two bowlfuls of lentils into the ashes. 'It's impossible.'

Ashputtel went out into the garden and called: 'Gentle doves and turtle-doves, all you birds of the sky, come and help me sort my lentils:

> Into the pot if they're nice to eat
> But swallow the bad ones with your beak.'

Once again, the white doves, then the turtle-doves, then all the many birds of the sky came skimming and swirling in and peck-peck-pecked all the good grains into the bowls. And this time, it wasn't even half an hour before they'd finished and flown out of the window. Ashputtel took the bowls straight to her stepmother, overjoyed at the thought of going to the feast. But her stepmother snapped: 'It's no good. You can't come because you haven't any fine dresses, you haven't any shoes, you can't dance and we'd all be ashamed of you.' And she turned her back on Ashputtel and swept off with her two proud daughters.

When everybody had gone and the house was empty, Ashputtel went to her mother's grave under the hazel-tree and called out:

> 'Shake your leaves and branches, little tree,
> Shower gold and silver down on me.'

And the white bird threw down a golden and silver dress and a pair of slippers embroidered in silk and silver. Quick as a smile, Ashputtel put it all on and hurried to the feast. She looked so beautiful in the golden dress that her stepsisters and stepmother couldn't see that it was Ashputtel and thought she must be a Princess from a foreign land. Ashputtel, they thought, even as they stared at this gorgeous girl, was crouched at home in the dirt, squinting, and picking lentils out of the ashes. The Prince came over to her, bowed deeply, took her hand and danced off with her. He wouldn't let go of her hand, or dance with anyone else; and if another man came up and asked her to dance, he said: 'She is my partner.'

Ashputtel danced till it was evening, and then she wanted to go home. But, because the Prince was desperate to find out whose beautiful daughter this was, he announced: 'I shall come with you and escort you home.' But Ashputtel managed to slip away from him and hid up in the dovecote. The Prince waited until her father came home, and told him that the lovely, mysterious girl had jumped into the dovecote. The father thought: 'Could she possibly be Ashputtel?' So he sent for the axe and the pick and broke into the dovecote. It was empty. Ashputtel had jumped down from the other side and run to the hazel-tree. She'd removed her gorgeous clothes and laid them on her mother's grave and the white bird had taken them away. Then she had crept back to the kitchen in her old grey smock. When the others came indoors, they saw only grubby little Ashputtel lying among the ashes in her dirty clothes, with a dim little oil-lamp flickering at the fireplace.

Next day, the second day of the feast, when everyone had left, Ashputtel went to the hazel-tree and said:

> 'Shake your leaves and branches, little tree,
> Shower gold and silver down on me.'

This time, the bird dropped down an even more splendid dress than before; and when Ashputtel arrived at the feast, everyone gaped wide-eyed at her beauty. The Prince had been waiting only for her. He took her by the hand immediately and danced with her and nobody else. 'She is my partner,' he said to any man who came near her. When evening came and it was time for her to leave, the Prince followed her, watching which house she would enter. But she managed to lose him and ran into the garden behind the house, where there was a fine big tree with pears growing on it. She shot up it, just like a squirrel, and hid in its branches; and the Prince hadn't a clue where she was. When her father came, he said: 'That strange, unknown girl has escaped me again. I think she must have jumped into this pear-tree.' The father thought: 'Could it possibly be Ashputtel?' So he sent for the axe again and chopped down the tree, but there was no one in it. And when they all went into the kitchen, there was Ashputtel curled up in her ashes as usual. She'd jumped down from the far side of the tree, given back her fine clothes to the white bird, and dressed in her grubby grey smock again.

On the third day, when her parents and stepsisters had left, Ashputtel went again to her mother's grave and spoke to the hazel-tree:

> 'Shake your leaves and branches, little tree,
> Shower gold and silver down on me.'

This time, the bird threw down a dress that was so sparkling and brilliant that the like of it had never been seen before; and the slippers were golden all over. When she appeared at the wedding-feast in this wonderful costume, everyone was speechless with admiration and wonder. The Prince danced only with her, and if anyone asked her for a dance, he said: 'She is my partner.' When evening came, Ashputtel wanted to leave, and, even though the Prince wanted to come with her, she dashed away from him so fast that he couldn't follow. But this time, the Prince had thought of a trick. He had had the whole staircase covered with tar, and as she rushed down it, her left slipper got stuck there. The Prince picked it up and looked at it closely. It was small and dainty and golden all over.

The next morning, the Prince took the slipper to the house of Ashputtel's father and said to him: 'I will only marry the girl whose foot fits into the golden shoe.' Ashputtel's two stepsisters were thrilled because they had beautiful feet. The eldest took the shoe up to her bedroom to try on, with her mother watching beside her. But the shoe was too small and she couldn't fit her big toe in. And then her mother handed her a knife and said: 'Slice off your toe. Once you're Queen you won't have to bother with walking.' The girl chopped off her toe and pushed her foot into the shoe. She gritted her teeth against the terrible pain and went back to the Prince. Seeing her foot in the golden slipper, the Prince took her as his bride and rode off with her on his horse. But their way took them past Ashputtel's mother's grave; and there were the two doves perched on the tree calling:

> 'Rookity-coo, Rookity-coo!
> There's red blood in the golden shoe.
> She chopped her toe, it was too wide,
> And she is not your rightful bride.'

The Prince looked at her foot and saw the blood oozing out. He turned round his horse and rode straight back to the house and said she was the wrong girl and that the other sister must try on the shoe. So the second sister rushed up to her bedroom and managed to squeeze her toes into the shoe, but her heel wouldn't fit. Her mother passed her the knife and said: 'Carve a slice off your heel. When you're Queen you won't need to walk anywhere.' The girl hacked off a piece of her heel and forced her foot into the shoe. Then she bit her lip against the awful pain and went back to the Prince. He took her as his bride, lifted her on to his horse and rode off. But as they passed the hazel-tree by the grave, the two doves were perched there and called out:

> 'Rookity-coo, Rookity-coo!
> There's red blood in the golden shoe.
> She chopped her heel, it was too wide,
> And she is not your rightful bride.'

The Prince looked at the foot and saw the blood seeping from the slipper and staining her white stocking crimson. So he turned round his horse and rode the false girl home. 'She's not the right one either,' he said. 'Have you got another daughter?' 'No,' said the man. 'The only other girl is a grubby little kitchen-maid whom my dead wife left behind her. She can't possibly be the bride.' The King's son asked for her to be sent for. 'No,' cried the stepmother. 'She's much too dirty. She's not fit to be looked at.' But the Prince insisted and Ashputtel had to appear. First, she scrubbed her face and hands quite clean, then went in and curtsied before the Prince. He handed her the golden shoe. Ashputtel sat down on a stool, took her dainty foot out of the heavy wooden clog, and slipped on the little slipper. Of course, it fitted her perfectly, and when she stood up and the Prince looked into her face he recognized her at once. She was the beautiful girl who had danced with him. 'This is my rightful bride!' he said. The stepmother and the two sisters were thunderstruck and turned ashen-faced with fury; but the Prince put Ashputtel on his horse and rode off with her. As they passed the hazel-tree, the two white doves sang out:

> 'Rookity-coo, Rookity-coo!
> A perfect foot in a golden shoe.
> Three times has the good Prince tried,
> And now he's found his rightful bride.'

When they had sung this, they flew down and perched on Ashputtel's shoulders, one on the left and one on the right, and there they stayed.

On Ashputtel's wedding-day, the two false sisters came, hoping to suck up to her and have a share in her good fortune. As the bridal procession was entering the church, the eldest sister was on the right and the younger on the left; and the two doves flew at them and pecked out one of each of their eyes. And as they were all coming out of the church, the elder sister was on the left and the younger on the right; and the doves swooped again and pecked out their other eyes. And so, because of their cruelty and deceit, they were punished with blindness for the rest of their days.

A Riddling Tale

Now picture this: three women were turned into flowers which grew in a field.

And one of them was allowed to spend each night in her own home.

But once, when her night was nearly over, and the day was coming, forcing her back to the field to be a flower again with her companions, she said to her husband: 'If you will come early this morning and pick me, I shall be set free. I will be able to stay with you for ever.'

So her husband did this.

The riddle of the tale is: How did her husband recognize her when all three flowers were identical?

Here is the answer: Because the wife was at home during the night, no dew fell on her, like it did on the other two.

And that is how her husband knew her.

The Mouse, the Bird and the Sausage

Once upon a time, a mouse, a bird and a sausage became friends. They set up house together and lived in perfect peace, happiness and prosperity. It was the bird's job to fly to the forest every day and bring back wood. The mouse had to fetch water, light the fire, and lay the table; the sausage had to do the cooking.

But those who don't appreciate how well off they are are always tempted by something different. One day, the bird met another bird in the forest, and told him all about his excellent circumstances in life. After he'd stopped his boasting, however, the second bird called him a fool to do all the hard work, while the other two obviously had it easy at home.

When the mouse had fetched the water and made up her fire, she went to rest in her little room until they called her to lay the table. The sausage stayed by the pot, made sure that the food was well cooked, and just before dinner-time, it rolled itself once or twice through the broth to give it extra flavour. When the bird came home and put down his load, they sat down at the table, and after a good meal, they slept well till the next morning. It really was a splendid life for them all.

But the next day, the bird, because of what the other bird had said, refused to go into the forest. He'd been their slave for long enough, he said, and they weren't going to make a fool of him any longer. It was time to change and arrange things in a different way. The mouse and the sausage pleaded with him; but in spite of all they said, the bird was determined to have his own way. So they drew lots to decide who would do what; and the result was that the sausage was to fetch wood, the mouse was to cook, and the bird was to draw water.

Now look what happened. The sausage went out to the forest for wood, the bird made up the fire, and the mouse put on the broth in the pot. Then the mouse and the bird waited for the sausage to come home with the wood. But the sausage was away for such a long time that they were both worried something had happened; and the bird flew out part of the way to search for it. Not far off, he met a dog who had decided the sausage was rightful prey, grabbed hold of it and eaten it. The bird accused the dog of daylight robbery, but it was all to no good. The dog just said he'd found forged documents on the sausage, so it deserved to die.

The bird sadly picked up the wood and flew home to tell the mouse what had happened. They were both very distressed, but agreed to make the best of things and to stay together. And so the bird laid the table and the mouse prepared the food. She decided she would flavour it by getting into the pot like the sausage used to do; but before she had even reached the middle of the vegetables, she lost her fur and skin and life in the attempt.

When the bird came to carry in their dinner, there was no sign of the cook. In his panic, the bird scattered wood everywhere, calling and searching, but the mouse couldn't be found. Because of the bird's carelessness, a fire had started and he rushed to fetch water to put it out. But the bucket fell into the well, and he fell in after it; and as he could not manage to get out again, he drowned there.

Iron Hans

There was once a King whose castle was next to a great forest which was full of all kinds of wild animals. One day, the King sent out a huntsman to shoot a deer for him; but the huntsman never returned. 'Perhaps he's had an accident,' said the King and sent out two more huntsmen to find him. But they didn't come back either. So on the third day, the King sent for all his huntsmen and ordered: 'Scour the whole forest, and don't stop searching till you find all three of them.' But none of these huntsmen returned, and not one of the pack of hounds they'd taken with them was ever seen again. From then on, no one dared to enter the forest. There it stood, dark and silent and empty, with only a solitary eagle or hawk flying over it occasionally.

After many years, a huntsman from another country came before the King. He asked to stay at his court and volunteered to enter the dangerous forest. The King was reluctant to allow this, saying: 'The forest is unlucky. You would do no better than all the others, I fear, and you'd never get out.' But the huntsman replied: 'Sir, I will go at my own risk. I am frightened of nothing.'

So the huntsman went into the hushed, gloomy forest with his dog. The dog quickly picked up a scent and followed it; but after running a few yards, it was standing in front of a deep pool and could go no further. Suddenly, a naked arm shot out of the water, grabbed the dog and dragged it under. When the huntsman saw this, he went back and got three men to come with buckets to bail the water out of the pool. When they had scooped deep enough to see the bottom, they discovered a wild man lying there. His body was the colour of rusty iron and his hair hung over his face right down to his knees. They tied him up with ropes and pulled him away to the castle. Everyone there was astonished to see the wild man; but the King had him locked up in an iron cage in the courtyard. It was forbidden, on pain of death, to open the door, and the Queen herself was to guard the key. From then on, everyone could visit the forest in safety.

The King had a son who was eight years old. One day, the boy was playing in the courtyard with his golden ball, when it bounced into the cage. He ran up to the cage and said: 'Can I have my ball back?' 'No,' answered the wild man. 'Not unless you open this door for me.' But the boy replied: 'No, I won't do that. The King has forbidden it,' and he ran away. The next day he came back and asked for his ball, and the wild man said: 'Open my door.' But the boy refused. On the third day, the King had ridden out to hunt, and the boy came again and said: 'I can't open your door even if I wanted to, because I don't have the key.' Then the wild man replied: 'It's under your mother's pillow; you can get it from there.' The boy was so anxious to have his ball back that he threw all sense and caution to the winds and fetched the key. The door was difficult to open and he hurt his finger doing it. When it was open, the wild man jumped out, tossed him his golden ball and hurried away. The boy was frightened now, and ran behind him crying: 'Oh, wild man, don't leave, or else I shall be beaten!' The wild man turned round, picked him up, put him on his rusty shoulders and strode quickly into the forest. When the King came home, he saw the empty cage and asked the Queen what had happened. She knew nothing at all about it and searched for the key, but it had disappeared. She called for her son, but he did not reply. The King sent his servants to hunt for him in the fields and countryside, but they could not find him. Everyone could guess what had happened and the whole court was bowed down with grief.

When the wild man was back in the dark forest, he took

the boy down from his shoulders and said to him: 'You will not see your mother and father again; but you can stay with me because you freed me, and I feel something for you. If you do everything I tell you to do, you shall get along fine. I have more gold and treasure than anyone else in the world.' Then he made a bed of moss for the boy to sleep on.

The next morning, the wild man took the boy to a spring and said: 'Look – this golden spring is as bright and clear as crystal. I want you to stay here and make sure nothing falls into it, or it will get polluted. Every evening I'll come back here to see if you have obeyed my instructions.' The boy sat down beside the spring. Sometimes he saw a golden fish or a golden snake in the water, and he was careful to let nothing fall in. After a while, his finger began to hurt so much that he dipped it into the water without thinking. He quickly pulled it out again, but saw that it had turned golden all over; and he couldn't wipe it off no matter how hard he tried. In the evening, Iron Hans came back and stared at him. 'What has happened to the spring?' he asked. 'Nothing, nothing,' said the boy, hiding his finger behind his back. But the wild man said: 'You have dipped your finger into the water. I'll let it pass this time; but make sure you don't let anything touch the spring again.'

At daybreak next morning, the boy was already sitting by the spring. His finger began to hurt him again. He rubbed it on his head and, by bad luck, a hair floated down into the spring. He pulled it out quickly, but it was completely golden. Iron Hans came back and he already knew what had happened. 'You have dropped a hair into the spring,' he said. 'I'll let you watch the spring once more, but if it happens a third time then the spring is polluted and you cannot stay with me any longer.'

On the third morning, the boy sat by the spring and didn't move his finger however badly it hurt him. But the time went very slowly, and he grew bored and began staring at his own reflection in the water. And as he leaned further and further over, trying to stare right into his eyes, his long hair tumbled down from his shoulders into the spring. He pulled himself up quickly, but all the hair on his head was already golden and shone like the sun. You can imagine how terrified the poor boy was! He took out his handkerchief and tied his hair up so that the man wouldn't see it. But when he came, he already knew what had happened, and said: 'Untie your handkerchief.' Then the golden hair streamed out, and although the boy tried to make excuses for himself, it was no good. 'You have failed the test and can stay here no more. Go out alone into the world and find out what poverty is like. But because you have a good heart, and I mean you well, I will permit you one thing. If you are ever in trouble, come to the forest and shout "Iron Hans!" and I will come and help you. My powers are great – greater than you know – and I have more gold and silver than I need.'

So the Prince left the forest, and walked along the highways and byways until at last he arrived at a great city. He looked for work there; but as he had learnt no trade, he could find none. In the end, he went to the palace and asked if they would have him. The courtiers didn't know what job to give him, but they liked him and let him stay. Then the cook employed him, getting him to carry wood and water and sweep out the ashes.

One day, when no one else was available, the cook ordered him to carry the food in to the royal table. Because he didn't want his golden hair to be seen, the boy kept on his hat. This had never happened in the King's presence before, and he said: 'When you serve at the royal table, you must take off your hat.' 'Oh, sir,' the boy answered, 'I can't. I've got terrible dandruff.' When he heard this, the King sent for the cook and told him off; asking him what he was thinking of to employ such a boy, and telling him to sack him at once. But the cook felt sorry for the boy and swapped him for the gardener's lad.

So now the boy had to work in the garden, even in bad weather; planting and watering and digging and hoeing. One summer's day when he was all alone, it was so warm that he took off his hat to get some fresh air on his head. The sunlight glistened and flashed on his golden hair, and the glittering rays came in through the Princess's window. She jumped up to see what it was, noticed the boy and called out to him: 'Boy! Bring me a bunch of flowers.' He quickly pulled on his hat, picked some wild flowers and tied them together. As he was carrying them up the steps, the gardener saw him and said: 'How can you take the King's daughter such common flowers? Go and find the prettiest and rarest you can for her.' 'Oh, no,' replied the boy. 'Wild flowers have the strongest perfume. She'll like these best.' When he got to her room, the Princess said: 'Take off your hat. It's rude to keep it on in my presence.' 'I can't,' he said again. 'I have dandruff on my head.' But she snatched his hat and pulled it off; and then his splendid golden hair cascaded down to his shoulders. He tried to run out, but the Princess held him by the arm and gave him a handful of sovereigns. He went away with them, but he didn't care about the gold. So he took them to the gardener and said: 'Here, these are a present for your children to play with.' Next day, the Princess again called to him that he was to bring her a bunch of wild flowers; and when he brought them she grabbed at his hat, but he held on to it firmly with both hands. She gave him another pile of gold coins, but he didn't want to keep them and gave them to the gardener again as toys for his children. On the third day, things were just the same – she couldn't pull off his hat, and he wouldn't take her gold.

Not long after this, the whole country went to war. The King gathered his troops together, not knowing whether he'd be able to stand up to the enemy army, which was far bigger in numbers than his own. Then the gardener's boy said: 'I am grown up now and want to fight in this war too.

Give me a horse.' The others laughed and said: 'Look for one when we've gone. We'll leave one behind in the stable for you.' When they had set off, he went to the stable and led out the horse. It was lame in one foot and limped – hobbledy-clop-clop-clop, hobbledy-clop-clop-clop. But he climbed on and rode away to the dark forest. When he came to the edge, he called out 'Iron Hans!' three times, so loudly that his voice echoed among all the trees. Suddenly the wild man appeared and said: 'What is your request?' 'I need a fine, strong horse, for I am going to war.' 'You shall have it, and you shall have even more than you ask for.' Then the wild man went back into the forest; and it wasn't long before a groom appeared, leading a powerful horse that snorted and pranced and neighed. Behind him, there followed a great troop of warriors, all in armour, their swords flashing in the sun. The youth gave his lame horse to the groom, mounted the warhorse and rode off at the head of his soldiers. When he arrived at the battlefield, many of the King's men had already fallen and the rest were close to defeat. The young man galloped up with his troops of iron, charging here and there among the enemy like thunder and lightning; and he struck down everyone who challenged him. They began to flee, but he chased them and fought on till there was not one of them left. Instead of going back to the King, though, he took his troops the back way to the forest and called for Iron Hans. 'What is your request?' asked the wild man. 'Take back your charger and your men in armour and give me back my lame horse.' All that he asked for was done, and soon he rode – hobbledy-clop-clop-clop – back home.

When the King returned to the palace, his daughter came to meet him and congratulated him on winning such a victory. 'It wasn't I who won,' said her father, 'but a strange knight who came to help me with his own soldiers.' His daughter wanted to find out who the stranger was, but the King didn't know and said: 'He chased after the enemy and

I never saw him again.' The Princess asked the gardener where his boy was, but he laughed and said: 'He's just limped back on his three-legged nag. The others have been teasing him and shouting out: "Here comes old hobbledy-nobbledy back again." They asked him, "Where have you been? Sleeping under a hedge all the time?" But he said: "I did better than all of you. Things would have been really bad without me." And they teased him and laughed at him even more.'

The King told his daughter: 'I will announce a great feast which will last for three days. You shall throw a golden apple, and perhaps the stranger will show himself.' When he heard about the feast, the young man returned to the forest and called Iron Hans. 'What is your request?' he asked. 'I want to catch the Princess's golden apple.' 'You practically have it already,' said Iron Hans. 'You shall also have a suit of red armour and ride on a magnificent chestnut horse.' When the day of the feast arrived, the young man galloped up to join the other knights, and no one recognized him. The King's daughter came forward and tossed a golden apple to the knights; but he was the only one who caught it, and as soon as he'd got it, he galloped away. On the second day, Iron Hans dressed him as a white knight on a white horse. Again he was the only one who caught the apple and, again, he galloped away with it. The King grew angry and said: 'This behaviour is disgraceful. He must come before me and tell me his name.' He gave orders that the knight was to be pursued if he rode away again, and he was to be attacked with swords if he would not return willingly.

On the third day, Iron Hans gave the young man a suit of black armour and a black horse; and again he caught the apple. But when he galloped away with it, the Kings's men chased him, and one of them rode close enough to pierce the youth's leg with the tip of his sword. He escaped from them in spite of this, but his horse reared so violently that his helmet fell from his head, and they could see his golden hair. They rode back and reported all this to the King.

The next day, the Princess asked the gardener about his boy. 'He's working in the garden. What a strange fellow he can be. He went to the feast and only arrived back last night. Then he showed my children three golden apples he had won.' The King had the gardener's boy summoned before him, and he came with his hat still on his head. But the Princess went straight up to him and pulled it off; and then his golden hair fell down to his shoulders and they were all amazed by his beauty. 'Are you the knight who came to the feast every day wearing different colours and who caught the three golden apples?' asked the King. 'Yes,' he replied, 'and here are the apples.' He took them from his pocket and gave them to the King. 'If you need more proof, sir, you can see the wound your men gave me when they chased me. But I am also the knight who helped you to defeat your enemies.' 'If you can perform such actions, then you are not a gardener's boy. Tell me now, who is your father?' 'My father is a rich and powerful King, and I have as much gold as I need.' 'I now see,' said the King, 'that I have a lot to thank you for. Is there anything I can do to please you?' 'Yes,' he answered, 'there certainly is, sir. Give me your daughter's hand in marriage.' When she heard this, the Princess laughed and said: 'Well, he doesn't waste his words, does he! But I knew from his golden hair that he wasn't a gardener's boy!' And she went up to him and kissed him.

His mother and father came to the wedding and were overjoyed, because they had already given up hope of ever seeing him again. And as they were all sitting at the wedding-feast, the music suddenly stopped, the doors burst open, and a magnificent King entered in great style. He went up to the young man, embraced him and said: 'I am Iron Hans. I was under a spell that turned me into a wild man – but you have set me free. All my treasure shall be yours.'

The Lady and the Lion

A merchant was about to go on a long journey, and when he was saying goodbye to his three daughters, he asked each of them what they would like as a present. The eldest asked for pearls, the second asked for diamonds, but the youngest said: 'Father, I would like a rose.' Her father said: 'Even though it's the middle of winter, if I can find one, you shall have it.'

When it was time for him to come home again, he'd found pearls and diamonds for the two eldest; but he had searched everywhere in vain for a rose. He'd gone into many gardens asking for one, but people had just laughed and asked him if he thought roses grew in snow. This upset him, because his youngest child was his favourite. He was travelling through a forest. In the middle was a splendid castle and around the castle was a garden. Half of it was in bright summer time and the other half in gloomy winter. On one side grew the prettiest flowers, but on the other everything was dead and buried in snow. 'What a blessing!' he said to his servant, and ordered him to pick a rose from the beautiful rose-bush there. But then, as they were riding away, a ferocious lion leapt out, shaking his mane and roaring so loudly that every flower in the garden shook. 'Anyone who tries to steal my roses will be eaten by me,' he roared. Then the man said: 'I'd no idea it was your garden. Please forgive me. What can I do to save my life?' The lion said: 'Nothing can save it. Only if you give me what you first meet when you go home. If you agree to do that, then I'll let you live. *And* you can take the rose for your daughter as well.' But the man hesitated and said: 'But it might be my youngest daughter. She loves me best and always runs to meet me when I get home.' His servant, though, was scared stiff and said: 'It might not be her. It could just as easily be a dog, or a cat.' So the man gave in, took the rose, and promised that the lion should have whatever he first met when he got home.

When he arrived home and went into his house, his youngest daughter ran up to him and kissed and hugged him. And she was delighted to see that he'd brought her a rose. But her father started to cry, and said: 'My darling child, this rose has cost too much. In exchange for it, I've promised to give you to a savage lion. When he has you, I'm sure he'll tear you to pieces and eat you.' He told her everything that had happened and begged her not to go. But she comforted him and said: 'Dear father, you must keep your promise. I will go there and make the lion gentle, so that I can come safely home to you.'

Next morning, she was shown the road and set off bravely for the forest. The lion, in fact, was an enchanted Prince. By day he and his people were lions; but at night they became humans again. When she arrived, she was treated kindly and taken to the castle. When night fell, the lion turned into a handsome Prince and their wedding was held with much celebration. They lived happily together but he came to her only when it was dusk and left her when morning drew near. After a while, his deep voice spoke to her from the darkness: 'Your eldest sister is getting married tomorrow and your father is holding a feast. If you would like to go, my lions will escort you there.' She said: 'Yes, I'd love to see my father again,' and set off in the morning with the lions. There was great joy and happiness when she appeared, because everyone thought she'd been torn to shreds and killed by the wild lion. But she told them her husband was a Prince, and how happy she was. She stayed with them till the feast was over, and then returned to the forest.

When her second sister was getting married, she was

invited again, and said to the Prince: 'I don't want to go alone this time. Come with me.' But he said it was too dangerous for him, and that he must never be exposed to light. He explained that if, when he was there, even a ray of candlelight fell on him, he would turn into a dove and have to fly about the world for seven long years. But she pleaded: 'Oh, do come with me. I will take special care of you and protect you from all light.' So they set off together with their little child.

She chose a room for him there, with walls so thick that no ray of light could get through. The Prince was to lock himself in there when all the candles were lit for the wedding-feast. But there was a tiny crack in the door that nobody noticed. The wedding was celebrated splendidly; but when the procession came back from church with all its bright, flickering candles, it passed close by his room. A ray as fine as a single hair fell on the Prince; and as soon as it touched him he was transformed. When she came to find him, there was only a white dove in the room. The dove told her: 'Now for seven years I must fly around the globe. But for every seventh step you take, I will shed one white feather. That will show you the way, and if you follow it you can set me free.' The dove flew out of the door. She followed him. And at every seventh step, a little white feather fell down faithfully and showed her the way.

So she walked and walked through the big wild world – never even resting – and the seven years were almost over. One day, no feather fell; and when she looked up, the dove had disappeared. She thought to herself: 'No one human can help me with this.' So she climbed up to the sun and said to him: 'You shine into every crack, over every mountain; have you seen a white dove flying?' 'No,' replied the sun. 'I have not. But I'll give you this casket. Open it when you are most in need.' She thanked the sun and walked on until it was evening. The moon rose and she asked her: 'You shine all night, over all the fields and the forests; have you seen a white dove flying?' 'No,' said the moon. 'I have not. But I'll give you this egg. Break it when you are in great need.' She thanked the moon and walked on until the night wind began to blow on her. She said to it: 'You blow on every tree and under every leaf; have you seen a white dove flying?' 'No,' said the night wind. 'I have not. But I'll ask the other three winds if they've seen it.' The east and the west winds came and had seen nothing; but the south wind breathed: 'I saw the white dove. It has flown to the Red Sea and has become a lion again, because the seven years are now up. The lion is fighting with a dragon, but the dragon is really an enchanted Princess.' Then the night wind said to her: 'Follow my advice. Go to the Red Sea. On the right bank you'll see some tall reeds. Count them, break off number eleven, and hit the dragon with it. Then the lion will be able to overpower it and both of them will become human again. When this happens, set off at once with your beloved Prince and travel home over land and sea.'

So the poor wanderer went on, and found everything just as the night wind had said. She counted the reeds by the sea, snapped off the eleventh, and struck the dragon with it. Then the lion subdued it and they both became human immediately. But when the Princess, who had been the dragon, was released from the spell, she seized the Prince by the arm and carried him off. The poor girl, who had followed and walked so far, sat down and wept. But in the end, she found her courage and said: 'I will still travel as far as the wind blows and as long as the cock crows until I find my love again.' And she set off along long, long roads until at last she arrived at the castle where the two of them were living together. She discovered soon there was going to be a feast to celebrate their wedding; but she said: 'Heaven will help me.' Then she opened the casket that the sun had given her. Inside was a dress as dazzling as the sun itself. So she put it on, and went up to the castle. Everyone stared at her in astonishment, even the bride. In fact, the bride liked the dress so much that she wanted it for a wedding-dress and asked if it was for sale. 'Not for money or land,' the girl answered, 'but for flesh and blood.' When the bride asked what she meant, the girl said: 'Let me sleep a night in the same room as the bridegroom.' The bride wouldn't agree; but she wanted the dress so badly that at last she said yes. But she told her page to give the Prince a sleeping-draught.

When it was night, and the Prince was already sleeping, the girl was led into his bedchamber. She sat on the bed and said: 'I have followed after you for seven long years. I have asked the sun and the moon and the four winds for news of you. I have helped you against the dragon. Do you really forget me?' But the Prince was fast asleep and only thought he heard the wind murmuring and rustling in the trees. When morning came, she was taken out of his room and had to hand over the golden dress. And because it had all been no use, she wandered sadly into the fields, sat down, and cried. While she was sitting there, she remembered the egg which the moon had given to her. So she cracked it open and out came a clucking hen with twelve little chickens made of gold. They ran about chirping and cheeping, then crept under their mother's wings. They were the most gorgeous sight anyone could see. She stood up and drove them through the field until the bride looked out of her window. The tiny chickens delighted her so much that she hurried down and asked if they were for sale. 'Not for money or land, but for flesh and blood. Let me sleep another night in the bridegroom's chamber.' The bride said yes, but she intended to cheat her like before. But when the Prince was going to bed, he asked the page what the murmuring and rustling in the night had been. Then the page told him everything: that he'd been forced to give him a sleeping-potion, because a strange girl had slept secretly in his room; and that he was supposed to give him another one tonight. The Prince said: 'Pour the sleeping-draught away.' At night, the girl was led in again; and when she started to tell him all the sad things that had happened and how faithful to him she had been, he immediately recognized the voice of his beloved wife. He jumped up and cried: 'Now I am really released! I have been in a dream, because the strange Princess has bewitched me to make me forget you. But heaven has sent you to me in time, my dear love.' Then they both crept away from the castle, secretly in the dark, because they were afraid of the strange Princess. Together they journeyed all the way home. There they found their child, who had grown tall and beautiful; and they all lived happily until the end of their days.

The Magic Table, the Gold-Donkey and the Cudgel in the Sack

It was no more than once upon a time there was a tailor who had three sons and one goat. The goat provided milk for the four of them; so every day it had to be taken out to graze, and fed well. The sons took turns in doing this. One day, the eldest son took the goat to the churchyard. There was lots of excellent greenery there and he let her graze and jump around. At dusk, when it was time to go home, he asked her: 'Goat, have you had enough to eat?' And the goat replied:

> 'I've had enough,
> I'm full of the stuff. Beh! Beh!'

'Let's go home then,' said the boy, and he took hold of her halter, led her back to her shed and tied her up safely. 'Well,' said his father, 'did you feed the goat properly?' 'Oh, yes,' said his son, 'she's had enough; she's full of the stuff.' But his father wanted to check for himself, so he went down to the shed, patted the precious goat, and inquired: 'Goat, are you sure you've had enough to eat?' The goat replied:

> 'There was no grass to eat
> Where he took me to feed.
> Hard stones on the ground
> Were all that I found. Beh! Beh!'

'What's this I hear!' thundered the tailor. He ran back up and said to his eldest son: 'You liar! Why did you tell me you'd given the goat enough to eat when you've let her starve?' In his fury, he grabbed his yardstick from the wall and thrashed his son out of the house.

Next day, it was the second son's turn. He picked a good place by the garden hedge with lots of fresh, succulent greenery; and the goat munched it right down to the ground. At home-time, the boy asked: 'Goat, have you had enought to eat?' and the goat answered:

> 'I've had enough,
> I'm full of the stuff. Beh! Beh!'

'Let's get home then,' said the boy, and he led her back and tied her securely in the shed. 'Well,' said his father, 'did you feed the goat well?' 'Certainly,' said his son. 'She's had enough; she's full of the stuff.' But the tailor went down to the shed to make sure; and said: 'Goat, have you had enough to eat?' The goat answered:

> 'There was no grass to eat
> Where he took me to feed.
> Hard stones on the ground
> Were all that I found. Beh! Beh!'

'The heartless big lump!' yelled the tailor. 'Letting such a fine animal starve!' And he ran up and seized his stick and beat his poor son out of the house.

Now it was the youngest son's turn, and he was determined to do things properly. He chose a spot with abundant leafy bushes and let the goat nibble away to her heart's content. In the evening, he asked: 'Goat, are you quite, quite sure you've had enough?' The goat replied:

> 'I've had enough,
> I'm full of the stuff. Beh! Beh!'

'Let's go home then,' said the boy, and he led her to her shed and tied her up. 'Well,' asked his father, 'have you fed the goat properly?' 'Yes,' said his son, 'she's had enough; she's full of the stuff.' But the tailor didn't trust him, and went down to ask: 'Goat, are you sure you've had enough to eat?' And the wicked goat said:

> 'There was no grass to eat
> Where he took me to feed.
> Hard stones on the ground
> Were all that I found. Beh! Beh!'

'You pack of liars!' roared the tailor. 'All three of you are deceitful and undutiful. Well, you'll not make a fool out of me any more!' And quite puce in the face with rage, he rushed up and thwacked the poor boy's back with the stick so hard that he ran out of the house.

Now the old tailor was all alone with his goat. Next morning, he went down to the shed, stroked the goat and said: 'Come along, my little pet, I'll take you out to graze myself.' He led her away to a place where there were green hedges and moist grasses and all the things goats love to eat. 'Now you can eat your fill for once,' he said; and let her chomp away till evening. Then he asked: 'Dear goat, have you had enough to eat?' And the goat replied:

> 'I've had enough,
> I'm full of the stuff. Beh! Beh!'

'Come along home then,' said the tailor; and he led her to her shed and tied her up. As he was leaving, he turned round and said: 'Now for once I *know* you've really had plenty to eat.' But he had no more luck with the goat than his sons had had; and the bad goat bleated out:

> 'There was no grass to eat
> Where you took me to feed.
> Hard stones on the ground
> Were all that I found. Beh! Beh!'

When the tailor heard this, he was horrified and realized how unjustly he'd treated his three sons. 'You ungrateful beast!' he screamed at the goat. 'Just you wait! I'll make a mark on you that'll stop you showing your treacherous face among respectable people!' He rushed upstairs, grabbed his razor, lathered the goat's head, and shaved it as smooth as a billiard-ball. And because the stick would have been too good for it, he fetched his whip and flogged her so badly that she went leaping away for her life.

So the tailor was now all alone in his empty house. He became terribly sad and longed to have his sons back again, but nobody knew where they were. The eldest boy had become a joiner's apprentice. He was hard-working and conscientious; and when his apprenticeship was over and it was time for him to move on, his master gave him a little table. It was made of wood and looked perfectly ordinary, but there was something special about it. If you put it before you and said 'Table, be laid!' this splendid little table would immediately cover itself with a clean tablecloth; and there would be a plate with a knife and fork, as many dishes of good hot food as there was room for, and a big, robust, glowing glass of ruby wine to warm the chilliest heart. The young man thought to himself: 'Now you've got enough for your whole life,' and he journeyed happily round the world. He didn't have to bother whether any inn he came to was good or bad or whether or not he could find a decent meal. Sometimes, if he was in the mood, he didn't even stay at an inn, but camped out in the fields and woods. He'd take the table from his back, set it before him and say 'Table, be laid!' and it gave him all the food and drink he wanted. Eventually, the boy decided to return home to his father. He thought: 'He won't be angry with me after all this time; and now that I have a magic table, he's sure to welcome me!' So he set off home, and one evening he came to an inn that was full of guests. They made him welcome and asked him to join them at their meal, otherwise there'd be no food left for him. 'No,' said the young joiner, 'I won't take your last few morsels. You shall be my guests instead.' They thought he was joking with them and they laughed. But he set down his table in the middle of the room and said: 'Table, be laid!' At once, it was covered with much better food than the landlord of the inn could even dream of, and the delicious smell of it made their noses twitch. 'Help yourselves, my friends,' said the joiner, and they all moved up their chairs, grasped their knives and forks, and tucked in happily. The amazing thing was that as soon as one dish was empty, another full one took its place immediately.

The landlord stood watching silently from a corner. 'I could do with a cook like that here at my inn,' he thought. The joiner and his guests ate and drank and laughed and talked late into the night. But finally they went to bed; and the young man lay down to sleep as well, putting his magic table against the wall. The landlord's envy kept him awake. He remembered that he had a table which looked exactly the same up in his attic. So very quietly he fetched it, crept in, and swapped it for the magic table.

Next morning, the joiner paid his bill, lifted the table on to his back – never dreaming that it was the wrong one – and set off for his father's house. He arrived home at midday and his father was overjoyed to see him. 'Well, well, well, my dear boy,' he said. 'What have you learnt?' 'Father, I've become a joiner.' 'That's a worthwhile trade,' replied his father, 'and what have you brought back from your travels?' 'Father, I've brought the most wonderful thing – a little table.' The old man examined the table all over and said: 'Well, you've made no work of art here. It's just a shabby old table.' 'But it's a magic table,' said the son. 'When I put it down in front of me and tell it to lay itself, the finest food and wine appear and gladden the heart. Just ask all our friends and relatives over and we'll give them a real treat. They can eat and drink as much as they want.'

So when all the guests had assembled, he put his little table in the middle of the room and said: 'Table, be laid!' But this table did nothing. It stayed just as bare and wooden and still as any other table that doesn't understand when it's spoken to. Then the poor joiner realized what had happened at the inn; and he stood there ashamed and embarrassed that everyone would think he was a liar. His relations had a good old laugh at him, but had to go home with empty stomachs. His father got out some cloth and went on tailoring, and the son went to work for a master joiner.

The second son had fetched up at a mill and apprenticed himself to the miller. When he'd finished his time, his master said: 'Because you've been such a good worker, I'm going to give you a donkey. He's very special. He doesn't pull a cart and he won't carry sacks of flour either.' 'Then what's the use of him?' asked the young man. 'He spits out gold,' said the miller. 'If you stand him on a cloth and say "Jobaloo", this magnificent creature will produce gold coins for you from both ends!' 'This is wonderful,' said the young man. And he thanked his master and set off into the world. If ever he needed gold, he only had to say 'Jobaloo' to his donkey. Out would pour a shower of gold coins and he just had to bend down and pick them up. Because his purse was always full of gold, he bought the best of everything. After travelling for a time, he decided to visit his father. He thought: 'When I turn up with the gold-donkey, he'll forget his anger and make me welcome.' On his way home, he stopped at the same inn as his brother. He was leading his donkey, and the landlord was about to take it for him, when he said: 'Don't bother yourself, landlord. I'll take my donkey to the stable myself. I like to know where he is.' The landlord thought this was strange, and that a man who had to tie up his own donkey wasn't likely to have much money to spend. But when the young man pulled two gold pieces from his pocket and told him to buy him something good for supper, the landlord opened his eyes wide and hurried away to buy the best food and drink. After dinner, his guest asked him if he owed him anything, and the greedy landlord thought he might as well charge double and asked for two more gold pieces. The boy put his hand in his pocket, but it was empty, so he said: 'Hang on, landlord, I'll just go and get some more gold.' But he took the tablecloth with him.

The landlord couldn't understand this at all, so he secretly followed the boy. He crept along and discovered that his guest had bolted the stable door. Filled with curiosity he peered in through a gap in the wood. The young man spread the tablecloth under the donkey, called out 'Jobaloo', and suddenly the beast began to throw out gold from both ends – showers and showers of it. 'Well, who would believe it,' said the landlord, rubbing his eyes in amazement. 'That's a quick way to make gold. I could use a moneybag like that.' The guest paid for his dinner and went to bed; but the landlord sneaked down to the stables overnight, led the gold-donkey away and tied up another donkey in its place.

Early next morning, the boy set off, thinking he still had his own gold-donkey. He arrived home at midday and his father gave him a warm welcome. 'Well, well, well, my boy, and what have you become?' 'I am a miller, father.' 'And what have you brought back with you from your travels?' 'Just a donkey.' 'We're all right for donkeys around here,' said the father. 'It would have been better if you'd brought a decent goat.' 'But this is no ordinary donkey, father, it's a gold-donkey. When I say "Jobaloo", this wonderful creature drops down a whole tablecloth of gold coins. Ask all our friends and relatives round and I'll make every one of them rich.' 'That'll do me,' said the tailor. 'I won't need to work my old fingers to the bone with this needle any more.' And he ran round himself and invited all their relations.

As soon as everyone was there, the son asked them to make a space, spread out a cloth and led in the donkey. 'Watch this everybody!' he said proudly, and called out 'Jobaloo!' But what landed on the white cloth was certainly not gold, and it was obvious that this donkey could produce no more than any other old donkey. The poor young miller was mortified. He knew that he'd been tricked and just had to apologize to his relatives, who trudged home as poor as they'd always been. So the old man had to take up his needle again and the boy had to get a job with a miller.

The youngest son had apprenticed himself to a turner, and because this is such a skilled trade, he took longest to learn it. His brothers wrote him a letter, telling him of their bad luck and how the villainous landlord had stolen their magic gifts on the night before they got home. When the young turner had completed his time and was setting out to travel, his master rewarded him for his fine, honest work with a sack. 'It's got a cudgel inside,' he said. 'Well, I can sling the sack over my shoulder and make good use of it,' said the boy, 'but the cudgel will just make it heavy to carry. What use is it?' 'Plenty use,' said his master. 'If anyone ever does you any harm at all, just say "Cudgel, out of the sack!" and the cudgel will jump out at whoever's there and dance so madly on their backs that they won't be able to walk for a week. And it won't stop till you say "Cudgel, back in the sack!" ' The young miller said thank you, slung the sack over his shoulder; and after that, if anyone gave him any trouble, he'd say 'Cudgel, out of the sack!' At once the cudgel would leap out and give their coats or jackets such a fierce dusting – while they were still wearing them – and it beat their backs so fast that before the next man knew what was happening it was his turn already.

Eventually, the boy arrived at the bad landlord's inn. He put his sack down in front of him on the table, and started to talk about all the miraculous things he'd seen on his travels. 'Oh yes,' he yawned, 'you come across magic tables and gold-donkeys and all that sort of thing – excellent in their way and I've nothing against them – but they're nothing compared to the treasure I've got in my sack here.' The landlord listened excitedly and wondered what it could be. He thought: 'Perhaps his sack is filled with jewels. If it is, *I* should have them as well. Twice is nice, but thrice is nicer.'

At bedtime, his guest lay down on the bench and put his

sack under his head for a pillow. When the landlord thought he was sound asleep, he sneaked up and began tugging very gently and slowly at the sack. His sly plan was to pull it out and put another one in its place. Of course, this was exactly what the turner wanted, and just as the landlord was about to give one last tug, he called out: 'Cudgel, out of the sack!' Quick as anger, the cudgel was out and giving the landlord a terrible dusting. The landlord screamed and howled, but the more noise he made, the more the cudgel danced on his back, till finally he fell to the ground and stayed there. Then the young man said: 'Unless you give back the magic table and the gold-donkey, the painful dance will begin again.' 'Oh no,' moaned the landlord – very humbly now – 'I'll give you the lot, sir, honestly – just tell that hideous thing to get back in its sack.' 'Very well, I shall give you mercy as well as justice,' said the young man, 'but just you mind your step in future.' Then he called out: 'Cudgel, back in the sack!' and the cudgel had a rest.

Next morning, the turner went home to his father with the magic table and the gold-donkey. His father was delighted to see him, and asked him what he had learnt. 'I am a turner, dear father,' he said. 'A very skilful trade,' said the old tailor. 'And what have you brought home from your travels?' 'Something very valuable, father. A cudgel in a sack.' 'A cudgel?' scoffed his father. 'What for? You can hack one off the nearest tree.' The son smiled. 'Not one like this, dear father; when I say "Cudgel, out of the sack!" the cudgel jumps out and bangs away at anyone who's giving me trouble. And it doesn't stop its bruising dance until they beg for mercy. Look, father, with this cudgel I've got back the magic table and the gold-donkey that were stolen from my brothers. So send for both of them and invite all our friends and relations. I'll fill their bellies with food and drink and their pockets with gold.' The old tailor still wasn't sure about this, but he did as his youngest son asked.

When they were all together, the turner put a cloth down

on the floor, led in the gold-donkey, and said to his brother: 'Now my dear brother, speak to your donkey!' The miller called out 'Jobaloo!' and there and then it began to rain gold coins on the cloth. The donkey didn't stop till everyone's pockets were bulging. (I bet you'd have liked to have been there too!) Then the turner fetched the little table and said: 'Speak to your table, my good brother.' As soon as the joiner cried 'Table be laid!' the table was crowded with every delicious dish and the best wine. Then they had a feast the like of which had never been known in the poor tailor's house, and the whole family stayed together till late at night, having the most wonderful party. The tailor locked away his needle and thread and yardstick, and lived long and happy and prosperous with his three fine sons.

But what about the wicked goat whose fault it was that the three sons had been thrown out of their home? Listen to this. She was so ashamed of being bald that she ran to a fox-hole and crawled in to hide there. When the fox came home, he saw two huge yellowy eyes gleaming at him in the darkness. He was so scared that he ran away. The bear met him and he looked so terrified that he asked: 'What's the matter, brother fox?' 'Oh,' said the fox. 'There's a terrible monster sitting in my earth-hole, glowering at me with glowing eyes.' 'We'll soon get rid of it,' said the bear, and he went with the fox to his hole and peeped in. But when he saw the fiery eyes, he was scared as well, and ran away. The bee met him, and saw that he looked upset and said: 'Bear, that's a very worried face you have. What's the matter?' 'Oh, it's awful,' said the bear. 'There's a savage beast with burning eyes sitting in brother fox's house and we can't get it out.' The bee said: 'Poor old bear. I know I'm only a little thing that you hardly ever notice, but I think I can help you.' The bee flew into the fox's hole, landed on the goat's bald head and stung her so badly that she leapt up bleating 'Beh! Beh! Beh!' and ran out into the big wide world like a mad creature. And no one knows where she ran to to this very day.